# Care
# Evolution

# Care
# Evolution

*Essays on Health as a Social Imperative*

Steven Merahn, MD

CONVERSATION
PUBLISHING

Printed in the United States of America.

First paperback edition June 2021.

10 9 8 7 5 4 3 2 1

Cover and layout design by G Sharp Design, LLC.

www.gsharpmajor.com

Cover painting: "Gram Stain" by Steven Merahn.

Excerpts from *Conceptual Revolutions in Twentieth Century Art* (Galenson DW Cambridge University Press 2009) reprinted with permission of the author.

ISBN 978-1-7359415-2-3 (paperback)

ISBN 978-1-7359415-3-0 (ebook)

Published by Conversation Publishing.

www.conversationpublishing.com

# Epigraph

*"New scientific ideas never spring from a communal body, however organized, but rather from the head of an inspired individual who struggles with his problems in lonely thought and unites all his thought on one single point which is his whole world for the moment."*

**Max Planck**

*"As long as there is poverty in the world, I can never be rich, even if I have a billion dollars. As long as diseases are rampant and millions of people in this world cannot expect to live more than twenty-eight or thirty years, I can never be totally healthy even if I just got a good checkup at Mayo Clinic. I can never be what I ought to be until you are what you ought to be. This is the way our world is made. No individual or nation can stand out boasting of being independent. We are interdependent."*

**Martin Luther King, Jr.**

*"No ideas but in things."*

**William Carlos Williams**

# Dedication

To my family:  CP, Alexander, David, Ellis, and Leah, all of whom, in your own ways, have encouraged me to be myself.

And to the generosity of spirit and commitment of educators, from elementary school through medical school, who got involved with me beyond the curriculum, without whom I would not be the person I am today.

# *Contents*

# The Social Imperative of Health

THIS BOOK IS based on a frightening occurrence: that there are opposing sides to the question as to whether we, as a society, want people to be sick or well. There are, in fact, individuals and organizations who are willing to use their power and influence to sustain avoidable suffering, disease, and disability by denying coverage, legislating barriers to accessing care, undermining the authority of healthcare professionals, and working to maintain networks of self-interest embedded throughout the healthcare ecosystem.

As a result, most of us face major healthcare events with doubt and confusion. We often find ourselves stranded without credible social constructs for healthcare and confronted by increasingly complex systems — often created by those without values that prioritize patients — with no clear sense of who is really in control of our care.

As we have seen during the COVID-19 pandemic, our systems of care are well equipped and can be mobilized to care for us in a medical crisis. However, the same pandemic has showcased the profound consequences of health-related social weaknesses, especially those we have chosen to ignore, such as systemic racism, social determinants of health, inequitable access to care, and deficient scientific literacy.

*There is a social imperative to equitably improve and sustain the quality of health of all citizens.*

This book is based on a singular premise: that there is a social imperative to equitably improve and sustain the quality of health of all citizens. Similar to the social imperatives we have adopted for security and literacy that manifest themselves in our systems of law enforcement and mandatory K-12 education, the social imperative for health is based on the evidence that preventing or attenuating health-related disruptions to work and family life improves educational and economic opportunity and the strength of our communities.

Just as there is value to society when everyone knows how to read, write, and comprehend basic numeracy, there is collective value from investments that *improve quality of health in order to enhance the capacity of individuals to succeed in the world on their own terms and contribute emotionally, socially, and economically as active, productive members of family and community.* In this case, the word "contribute" is based on the broad Merriam-Webster definition, meaning "to participate in the achievement or provision of something."

Similar to efforts to maintain ideological neutrality in our systems of education, the social imperative of health does not presume any specific value systems or political orientation in an individual's contribution; it may be purely personal or involve the lives of others. The social imperative only presumes that there is value to the community and society-at-large in preventing otherwise avoidable suffering, morbidity, and disability, as well as in supporting citizens to succeed in the world on their own terms.

While we have started to acknowledge inequities in law enforcement and education, and achieving the vision for those social imperatives remains a work in progress, the shared value of, and responsibility for, those infrastructures remains largely undisputed.

That said, with regard to the health of our citizens, we do not have a parallel commitment.

There is little doubt that access to healthcare can change lives. Regular access to healthcare improves self-reported health status, as well as a range of positive health behaviors, including preventive measures, more balanced resource utilization, and lower mortality rates for adults and children. Access to care is also associated with improved financial stability and educational and economic opportunities for individuals and families. A secure, literate, and healthy citizenry is the power that drives a strong economy.

However, even in the face of improved access, there remain significant healthcare disparities among millions of Americans, whose health and well-being are far below quality standards. Neither the adoption of information technologies nor expanded access to coverage has demonstrated the value of improved patient outcomes and quality of health.

Despite declarations of commitment to patient-centered care, the fact is that our systems of care remain firmly grounded in the traditional medical model, which is dominated by a focus on diagnoses, medication lists, and testing. It generally excludes functional status, social/emotional well-being, and personal growth from its architecture and organizing principles of care. Even recent interest in social determinants of health is driven by their influence on revenue models based on utilization management, not by a primary effort to improve quality of life in our communities.

Our current systems of care have no rational basis for their organizational or operational structure; they are designed by historical vestige and could not pass even the most superficial evidence-based tests.

Research confirms that our current approach to clinical care contributes only 10-20 percent to health outcomes and longevity. Behavior, lifestyle, social, and environmental factors contribute 50-60 percent — the largest effect — to the quality of health of individuals and communities.

In other words, the quality of health of our nation's citizens and communities, and the costs of caring for them, is more dependent on what we believe, and how we behave and live together, than on access to hospitals and medications. Our health would be better served by economic and emotional investments that repair the integrity of our communities and our capacity, as a national community, to commit to behaviors that contribute to common good.

Despite these facts, any effort toward productive change in healthcare is met by an exaggerated commitment to protecting current organizing principles, operating practices, and the vested self-interest of professional and commercial communities. An extraordinary amount of energy is expended in today's healthcare system defending inappropriate boundaries, which only results in persistent fragmentation in care systems.

The fact of the matter is that the American healthcare system is beyond any attempt to reform or repair it. Crafting, proposing, and implementing revisions of the current system has proven to be a waste of time. Quality, outcomes, the patient experience, and, most importantly, the ability to deliver highly reliable care deteriorate with each wave of reform. We've tried and failed with innovation, transformation, and disruption.

It's time to reconsider the fundamental organizing principles of our systems of care.

## *Burning Down the House*

While individuals within systems can try to overcome some systemic inequities, systems themselves are insulated structures designed to affect and sustain themselves, which includes their inherent bias. Only systemic change can genuinely eliminate bias and support true equity and inclusion.

There are two levels of bias in healthcare. One is inherent to healthcare, and the other is inherent to society but affects healthcare.

Healthcare-inherent bias is represented by the reductionist biomedical model, which focuses on disease over well-being, academic privilege, and medical paternalism. The societal biases that are systemic in healthcare include racial inequities and patriarchy.

Under these circumstances, sometimes a force of nature is required to move things along.

There are some lessons here if we consider healthcare as an ecosystem.

Ecosystems that grow in complexity until they achieve a steady state and become self-perpetuating are sometimes referred to as "climax communities" — a reference to their having reached a pinnacle of maturity.

Climax communities often resist change; the interactions between the members of the community become so intricate and interrelated as to prevent the admission of new species (or ways of being). The forces of maturity are so strong that when stressed, the community desperately attempts to achieve equilibrium and impede evolutionary progress, even when equilibrium is impossible, and change is unavoidable.

At a fundamental level, our healthcare ecosystem has all the characteristics of a climax community.

As a climax community, our healthcare ecosystem continues to preferentially select those "species" (disciplines, roles, mental models, and cultural mores) based on their "fit" and ability to sustain it. This is supported by a parallel evolutionary construct of *convergence*, which is where otherwise unrelated species must evolve similar phenotypical features (like white coats, the biomedical model, or respectability politics) in order to survive; species that don't converge are forced out (or into extinction).

While evolution is generally considered to be a gradual process in which interactions with the environment shape generational changes in species (or generate new species), ecosystems that resist evolutionary forces are less able to adapt to changing environmental conditions. As such, destruction events will ultimately force the opportunity for "ecological succession."

Notwithstanding the admonitions of Smokey the Bear, sometimes forest fires can be a good thing. Fire, as a natural phenomenon, is ecologically important; it serves to cleanse and rejuvenate an ecosystem (such as an entrenched climax community). While such fires also pose severe risks to property and life, it's us humans that have imposed ourselves on those environmental ecosystems—they are just doing what comes naturally to them. There are even cases where preventing or intervening in forest fires can increase the risk to both the ecosystem and local communities.

Putting aside the reality of fire's devastating potential, there are some lessons healthcare can learn from its ecological value and role in the productive evolution of ecosystems.

Three key concepts underlie the value of destruction in ecosystems: **nutrient cycling, diversity maintenance, and habitat structure**. It turns out that these concepts compose the critical triad of barriers that prevent the productive evolution of our capacity to improve the health of individuals and communities.

## 1.   Nutrient Cycling

Nutrients are elements necessary for survival, growth, and production. Nutrient cycling refers to a process by which these fundamental elements are transferred and exchanged within an ecosystem. When these elements are tied up in existing structures dedicated to survival and production, they are otherwise unavailable to nourish and promote growth.

Destruction forcibly releases nutrients into the ecosystem as raw materials for the evolutionary process to build upon, where they can be reclaimed, repurposed, and recycled to drive change.

## 2.  Diversity Maintenance

The science of ecology has shown us that the most diverse communities are the healthiest communities; the relationship between species diversity and community stability highlights the need to maintain the greatest richness possible within communities.

In ecosystems, diversity is more than just presence; it's full inclusion in the function of the ecosystem. Maintaining diverse populations is important to avoid premature convergence of an ecosystem. Ecosystems with limited diversity are less able to adapt to changing environmental conditions. Yet climax communities (like our current systems of care) resist change by preventing the admission of new species or by suppressing diversity of (and within) species.

In evolutionary biology, fitness in an ecosystem is determined by environment, the habitat structure, and the well-adapted community into which a new species seeks its place. Without changes in the environment, species diversity is impossible. Destruction events open the door to new species having the opportunity to find their place in the ecosystem. Some current members of the population adapt; others will not survive.

### 3. Habitat Structure

Habitat structure directly influences the diversity, richness, and composition of our communities. While habitat typically refers to physical environment, habitat also refers to the interconnected environments — physical, virtual, and social — in which healthcare is delivered. This includes our systems of government, public services, media, healthcare, and other social structures such as standards of respectability. In addition, habitat structure directly influences the diversity, richness, and composition of species assemblages. Community assembly, species coexistence, and the maintenance of biodiversity are all habitat dependent. Habitat structure can be used to sustain the oppression and discrimination of individuals and groups.

In particular, the emergence of urgent care as a new habitat structure, which arose from a failure of the climax community to respond to environmental changes related to behavior patterns in the community of service, exemplifies the role of habitat dynamics in moderating ecosystem processes and evolutionary potential.

## *From Vision to Reality*

There are many structures in the current healthcare ecosystem that prevent nutrient cycling, oppose diversity, and maintain habitat structures that prevent productive evolution.

These negative forces not only sustain the oppression and discrimination of individuals and groups based on assigned identities, but also the oppression of, and discrimination against, new ideas, new roles, and change in general. Disassembling these structures might:

- **Permit nutrient recycling to make resources available to marginalized communities that improve the health of those communities.**

- **Support collaboration models independent of role-based hierarchies; resisting convergence as a measure of fitness might allow new ideas to positively influence our systems of care.**

- **Eliminate discipline-based niches (departments, professional associations) and academic privilege that sustain existing habitat structures that reduce diversity (such as peer review where "peers" are narrowly defined).**

We must face the facts. Fundamental change is necessary. In evolutionary ecology, "destruction events" open the door to new species having the opportunity to find their place in the ecosystem. Some current members of the population adapt; others may not survive. In healthcare, if we are to achieve the social imperative of true equity and inclusion, not every practice should be preserved, not every habitat protected.

However, we can avoid crises associated with destruction events by actively disassembling the structures that function to support and sustain harmful social constructs. Such an effort will allow for a more stable and successful ecosystem; while some members of the population may have to adapt, the benefits of such diversity accrue to everyone and support a more productive and positive future for the ecosystem.

The systems that support achievement of the social imperative must *embrace* the multidimensional state that is humanness and acknowledge and reward the value of human aspirations, connection, and commitment.

This book explores elements associated with the evolution of healthcare as a system and the "species" that populate it. The purpose is to lay out an aspirational vision for the health of our nation based on a social imperative that provides a framework and the organizing principles of care necessary to make that vision a reality.

It's easy to say we want all people to be well. But to achieve the value of the social imperative, we must *actively change* the way we are organized and operate. We must evolve.

# 1

# Bringing Words to a Knife Fight: Why We're Losing the Healthcare War

EVERY WEEK, I read with great interest the viewpoints, perspectives, analysis, commentary, blog posts, and other dispatches from my peers and colleagues who are seeking to understand and influence both the current and future state of both our healthcare professions and our systems of care.

With each reading, I am reminded of the published words of my late mentor, Dr. Carleton Chapman, a former dean of Dartmouth Medical School and one-time president of the Commonwealth Fund: "…. our present scheme…for medicine is intellectually deficient, wasteful of money and time, and in urgent need of overhaul."

Because, despite decades of academic, economic, clinical, and governmental expertise, as well as the intellectual rigor of healthcare subject matter by policy experts, the vast majority of disciplined analyses and insights ring remarkably hollow.

*Healthcare is at war, and it's time the healthcare community realizes that our historical approach to using the realm of ideas to shape our future is a failure.*

Healthcare is at war, and it's time the healthcare community realizes that our historical approach to using the realm of ideas to shape our future is a failure. The passivity and genteelism illustrated in our approach reflects the weakness of our tools and techniques. Our enemies do not respect the rules of engagement; they are laughing at us.

Over the last few decades, the healthcare professional community has been battered by many forces of change, though none so powerful as the competition for our economic and social capital.

We have been largely destabilized and rendered vulnerable to those with selfish agendas: commercial and political communities unimpeded by the cultural and academic mores that comprise the historical underpinnings of the medical profession.

Dr. Arnold Relman, former editor-in-chief of the *New England Journal of Medicine*, called it the "medical-industrial complex," which has disintermediated and dehumanized the traditional doctor-patient relationship, undermined professionalism, and offloaded administrative responsibilities and costs to the healthcare delivery system without proportionate compensation.

We have tried to fight the battle, but the rules of engagement of politics and the free market are largely foreign to our professional culture and skill set.

The effort ended up driving a bigger wedge into the professional community. Physicians organized around specialty identities and entered a zero-sum game, with primary care and specialist physicians bickering over how dollars are divided among themselves as payers doled them out.

This fragmentation, pitting healthcare professionals against one another, only served to weaken us more, with patients losing trust as we were distracted and suffering reductions in our capacity to share the work of worrying about their health.

Physician-poet William Carlos Williams wrote, "No ideas but in things." Meaning is in the tangible; objects over concepts. I can tell you that the opposition has mastered the power of Williams's insight. They are not shaping the world with words, but with pervasive action. They have, and use with aplomb, skills and competencies that actively shape the knowledge, attitudes, and behavior of key target audiences toward their oft-hidden "prime directive" of protecting and growing their money and power. They are master manipulators that use every systemic weakness to their advantage.

Academics, researchers, and policy wonks fall right into the trap they set. Knowing our reductionist tendencies, they get us head-down in the details, trying to find the flaws, trying to understand the language, codes, and modeling scenarios. While we're distracted, they remove all our furniture without the need for stealth. Behind the curve and forced to react to an aggressive hand, we waste valuable brain power analyzing smokescreens.

We've seen this happen for decades, with healthcare communities reacting by trying to fight the battle of professional devaluation on economic terms. Unfortunately, trying to fight on other people's terms is almost always a losing proposition.

What is missing is any sense of goal-directed strategy. For all the experience and opinions out there, there are few insights as to how to wrest control of healthcare to the benefit of the health status of Americans, independent of partisan politics and lobbyists, in the same way the taxi industry was forever changed: not with an app, but with a strategy that uncoupled tradition and organized collective action.

It's time to embrace and master the very same weapons that I watched the opposition use against us (and in my decades of work in healthcare communications, helped them use against us): strategic thinking, communications discipline, audience targeting, message segmentation, value proposition, and economic leverage.

However, before this is possible, we need to organize and rally around a singular decisive inflection point: redefining the foundational identity of healthcare professionals, independent but inclusive of all disciplines and competencies — medicine, nursing, pharmacy, psychology, social work, therapists — and reclaiming these professions.

## *Identity and Value*

Confirming our commitment to excellence and human service beyond economics will revitalize the experience of care for patients and professionals and garner the affinity and loyalty necessary to assert our social and political will.

Two forces are in our favor. The first is the evolutionary principle, as described by Edmund O. Wilson, that "within groups, selfish individuals beat altruistic individuals, but groups of altruists beat groups of selfish individuals."

This means that if healthcare professionals organize around and commit to their fundamentally altruistic professional mission, we will have a better chance of winning the battle for professional identity than if we keep trying to compete on goals of specialty-based self-preservation.

This shift away from primary defense of economic status will be offset by the second force in our favor: the free market. It is also well established that people will pay a premium for what they perceive as value; the Ford Taurus you rent from Avis is exactly the same car you can get from Budget, yet people will pay a premium for Avis because they add value by reducing the "friction" — standing in line, dealing with customer staff, and other administrative burdens — associated with a car rental.

By regaining control over professional identity, healthcare professionals will have the opportunity to wrest control of the definition of value, and in doing so, revalue themselves in society and the marketplace.

One of the tenets of public relations is "define yourself before others define you." However, in many ways we are our own enemy, as clear definitions are impeded by our own tendency to asymptotically study issues without ever reaching a consensus upon which to build actionable insight; in this we squander our own time, energy, and knowledge as power.

"Needs further study" is not a strategy, but a platform from which to watch others overrunning our territory (note well: the ascendance of urgent care is a failure of mainstream medicine to recognize the changing dynamics of work and family life; would it have been so hard to have office hours till 9 p.m.?) According to a 2001 Institute of Medicine report, it takes an average of seventeen years before standard patient care is changed as a result of a significant research finding. How many times does something need to be studied before we declare that relationship valid and actively integrate it into our model of care?

Collective action could flip the subordinate position of professionals in the power structure of healthcare and wrest control of its evolution.

Why not adopt a model of collective care and a universal framework for care planning that would allow us to determine the requirements and value of investments to ensure that every member of society has the same opportunity to optimize their health status? We don't need to ask permission to do so.

Many disciplines and industries outside of healthcare have demonstrably powerful knowledge and tools that might productively contribute to the healthcare community's goals for improving the quality of care delivered to individuals and the quality of health of populations. Despite our capacity to master complex science and make life-changing — and potentially life-taking — decisions and actions, we may not necessarily be competent enough to evaluate the value and power of concepts from outside of healthcare, resulting in unconscious but significant bias in their selection, approval, and support. This phenomenon may be equally true for peer review, influencing what we do and do not see in our professional publications.

You can't see the whole picture with blinders on.

The big question is whether we, as a society, want people to be sick or well. The healthcare war is fought over who is best suited to educate about and influence that decision.

We are in a battle for control of the health of our communities at the system, societal, and individual levels. However, we cannot allow traditional academic mores to impede our progress in shifting the balance of power over the distribution (and control) of economic and other resources to those whose values prevail towards patient and community. We must be unified in message and aggressive in our communications strategies to enlist support and engage and activate the individuals and communities we serve.

# 2

# Sorry, Dr. Flexner: Revisiting Modern Medicine's Organizing Principles

ONE OF THE greatest strengths and most vulnerable weaknesses of the American medical system is our commitment to subject-matter expertise as a dominant organizing principle. Departments and service lines are organized by discipline, professional identities prevail along specialty or disciplinary lines, and career advancement is often associated with mastery defined by peer-review.

However, beyond the self-interest of the disciplines themselves, is there an objective, evidence-based need for departments of medicine, surgery, nursing, or any discipline-based departments? Is there a parallel need for department chairpersons? If there were no discipline-based departments, what would the relationship between professional disciplines look like? What would be the organizing principles of care? What would be the organizing principles of management? What would be the career paths?

*Responsibility for one of the biggest weaknesses of America's healthcare system rests with the people who run it.*

So, what to do? Is there any reason to keep the organizing principles of medicine we have inherited from the past? Confucius was quoted as saying, "Real knowledge is to know the extent of one's ignorance." If this is true — and in healthcare, it is — then responsibility for one of the biggest weaknesses of America's healthcare system rests with the people who run it.

When challenged to add new capabilities to our systems of care, the common solution is to find new experts and create new independent domains, like extra wings or additions to the house of medicine that are led by Department Chairs. This exemplifies our conceptualization of leadership. New units also have single leaders, such as Chief Quality Officers, or the spate of newly minted Chief Experience Officers across the country, or the recent posting for a Chief Respect Officer by a major academic health system.

Under this single-leader unit model, teamwork is really group work, in which all necessary domains are represented, and members work in parallel on tasks that match their purview. Achievement of individual goals among the members is expected to add up to the group's purpose. Final accountability is largely at the unit-leader level: chief-to-chief.

However, *interdisciplinary* is not synonymous with integrated, and modern challenges to healthcare — value-based care, social determinants of health, resource management, outcomes measures — are stress-testing the strength of healthcare's traditional organizing principles. Notions like experience management and respect cannot be realized solely by giving them a seat at the table. They must serve as a foundation for the design and construction of any system of behaviors or operations.

Outside of healthcare, there are well-established and powerful models for integration and collaboration in support of mission-critical, high-volume tasks, especially where there is extraordinary complexity or performance expectations (think Apple); where ill-defined or asymmetric problems emerge rapidly, requiring an organizational response under high risk conditions (think Army); or when orchestrating relational and logistic interactions to achieve engagement, affinity, and behavioral activation (think Universal Studios).

High-performance goal achievement in mutable environments characterized by complexity and diverse human factors requires sharing responsibility, authority, and accountability for achieving results. This represents an entirely new model of collective leadership for healthcare, based on a belief that benefits of collaboration will offset costs such as loss of autonomy and territorial control. Under this model, leaders actively coordinate and integrate their activities to effectively resolve unique, intricate, and dynamic problems that have dire consequences in the face of failure. Thus, leadership becomes a collective enterprise, as opposed to a departmental command-and-control phenomenon.

*Leadership becomes a collective enterprise, as opposed to a departmental command-and-control phenomenon.*

In healthcare, evolving from a directed, siloed, function-oriented culture to an interdependent culture with cross-functional and cross-organizational collaboration at its core will require a fundamental change in our organizing principles and operating model.

Eckert reminds us that implementing collective leadership requires both organizational transformation and the reimaging of traditional roles and perspectives on professional identity. Under collective leadership — whether for the care of an individual patient, enterprise adoption of new behavioral topographies, or organizational transformation — individuals, even if otherwise unaffiliated, organize into resource communities based on goal-driven functional requirements. These resource communities define and secure mutual agreement as to the intent and purpose of any initiative among all the relevant domain experts. Leadership is fluid, based on task-relevant skills and expertise, with explicit norms around a) structuring the team to assure its performance capabilities are aligned with mission and charter, b) establishing team norms, such as communication, information sharing, and work process, and c) shaping collaborative performance, monitoring and regulating its network functions and affective climate. To support situations where multiple issues are active in parallel, all team members agree to mores for team culture that transcend status in domain-based communities. This isolates tactical, goal-directed interactions from team-based governance interactions in order to maintain functional focus on the mission and have any role-based conflict managed off the playing field.

With that, the team is organized and operating around a mutual set of goals, strategic working principles, and an experience design.

Books like *If Disney Ran Your Hospital* miss a critical point: people expect good service from Disney, but that's not what drives their desire, motivates their participation, or defines the benefit of the experience. The real power of knowledge transfer from immersive entertainment into healthcare is not in the hospitality that takes place in the space before, between, or after direct care. Its power is in the capacity to inherently design systems of care that energize and support activation, engagement, and connection between patients and professionals in order to orchestrate and optimize transformative health-related experiences. Under this model, patient satisfaction becomes a secondary benefit of aligned expectations for the process and quality of care.

Revitalizing the experience of care for both patients and professionals in addition to improving the quality of health of our patients and communities will require us to evolve from domain-driven organizing principles to a clinical operating model that is focused on the collective management of multi-threaded interactions — at the system, role, and person-levels — and makes mastery of tactile and emotive performance as much a part of the profession of medicine as knowledge of anatomy and cell biology.

## *Medical Education and the Social Imperative*

Medicine is the science of solving human problems. Training in medicine demands a balanced understanding of science, problem-solving, and what it means to be human. The Flexnerian overemphasis on basic science — a contextual response to the lack of standardized curriculum and growth of undisciplined proprietary medical schools in the early 20th century — no longer serves the needs of professionals or patients. A goal of medical training is to expose students to materials in a way that will be made to count in their thinking for the rest of their lives. The teaching and learning of structure, rather than simply the mastery of facts and techniques, is crucial to the transfer of the learning problem that is central to the process of medical education.

Medical education reform is not about pedagogy, but about the mental model for health and a scope of practice that is not narrowly focused on biomedical determinants but is based on a) powerful models for complex, multidimensional problem-solving in the face of the variation and uncertainty that characterize humanness and b) expanding perspectives on interventions to all levels of being that are determining or influencing an individual's quality of health.

A medical school curriculum in service of the social imperative would expand the concept of basic science to integrate core concepts of multidimensional problem-solving and the human experience and use the framework of systems-theory to tie molecular, behavioral, and social events into a contact context as levels of being. To emphasize the dynamic nature of human development, medical school should not start with adult human anatomy, but genetics, conception, and fetal development. Here is a model framework for the first two years of such a medical education program:

| A Systems Framework for Health and Illness | Conception, Pregnancy and Fetal Development | Nervous System and Human Behavior | Human Systems in Health and Illness | |
|---|---|---|---|---|
| | | Anatomy | Physiology | Pharmacology |
| | | Histology | | |
| Genetics and the Genome | Molecular Biology and Cell Science | Etiologies of Disease and Methods of Medicine | | Introduction to Clinical Medicine II |
| Introduction to Clinical Medicine I | Health Systems: Organization, Structure and Function | Problem-Solving and Evidence-Based Practice | Clinical Information Systems | |

From a learning design perspective, the curriculum would be conceptually integrated, reflecting the importance of knowledge structure and content architecture in both learning and transfer of training to real-time, problem-solving environments. This would be supported with a special focus on the development of professional identity, clinical skills, judgment, and critical thinking skills, and a special focus on collaboration as a professional discipline.

## Healthcare and Social Evolution

While the evolution of 20th-century healthcare was characterized by breakthroughs in the understanding and management of molecular and cellular systems, the evolution of 21st-century healthcare has been seriously impeded by resistance to change in the design and operation of the systems that function and interact to deliver care.

Despite this resistance, the interactions between people, places, programs, and partners are being transformed, driven by a global pandemic and a combination of economic and policy forces, often without values that prevail towards patients or community, or consideration as to how unconscious bias shapes the new configurations that emerge from the evolutionary process.

This passive evolution can leave patients and communities stranded without credible social constructs for healthcare, confronted by increasingly complex systems with fluctuating loci of control and forced to face major healthcare events with doubt and confusion.

For some insight into this, let's look to history.

*The evolution of 21st-century healthcare has been seriously impeded by resistance to change in the design and operation of the systems that function and interact to deliver care.*

# Railroads, Newspapers, and Social Evolution

In 1950, life looked good for the US railroad system. After nearly 100 years of dominating American transportation, the railroads had seven times the intercity passenger-mile traffic of the commercial airline industry, which at the time was only thirty years old.

By 1970, however, the tables had turned. Airline services were carrying passengers nine miles for every mile traveled by railroads, which ended up bankrupt and nationalized; on balance, the proportion of passenger traffic maintained by intercity buses remained unchanged during this time.

While many forces drove this change — the Interstate Highway System, the familiarity and comfort of returning WWII veterans with airplane travel — one of the biggest failures of the railroad industry was the way it defined itself.

The identity of "railroad people" was tied to the history and mythology of the railroads: rolling stock, rights of way, scheduling, whistles. What they failed to realize was that they were actually in the *transportation business.* If they had done so, perhaps they would not have created an artificial barrier which placed airplanes outside their operational frame of reference and ignored them as a potential threat to their survival. If they had done so, they might have invested in airlines and modified their rail service strategies based on market forces, allowing a more productive evolution of their industry. In the end, hubris and legacy thinking blinded them to the reality of social dynamics.

This phenomenon was largely repeated forty years later by newspapers, when the internet emerged as a competitor to the print publishing industry. It now looms prominently over the American healthcare system.

*In the end, hubris and legacy thinking blinded them to the reality of social dynamics.*

As one historical reference on rail transformation notes, "An entire generation of rail managers had been trained to operate under (a restrictive) regulatory regime...Labor and their work rules were likewise a formidable barrier to change."

We could say the same thing about healthcare: "An entire generation of healthcare leaders had been trained to operate under an increasingly restrictive economic model. The culture of academic medicine and the existing operating model for care delivery were likewise formidable barriers to change."

## *How We Arrived at Healthcare's Current Dead End*

Over the last few decades, healthcare has been buffeted by many forces of change, but none so powerfully as the competition for its economic and social capital.

Our systems of care have been largely destabilized and rendered vulnerable to those with less selfless and less generous agendas: a commercial community unimpeded by the cultural and academic mores that have been the historical underpinnings of the medical profession. The "medical-industrial complex" took advantage of this vulnerability by increasing unpredictability in fee schedules, offloading administrative responsibilities and costs to the healthcare professional community, creating conflicts of authority around medical necessity, and disrupting the traditional doctor-patient relationship.

Once upon a time, there were well-defined, socially accepted modes of interaction between patients, healthcare professionals, and healthcare institutions. At a superficial level, patients (and hospital administrators for that matter) accepted physician authority without question and in exchange, physicians would shoulder the whole "work of worry" about a patient's health. While this model had its own flaws, it left the social structure of healthcare more certain. It was from this social compact — a balance of singular authority and mutual commitment — that patients felt they could move through difficult times with confidence. Physicians shouldered the risks, both professional and economic, for patient care.

While the paternalism of the old model is unacceptable in modern society, the historical social compact had a sense of wholeness and integrity that was comfortable and comforting to patients and community, providing a central figure grounded in the community who accepted us in the face of imperfection and offered a professional form of unconditional love and its associated commitments.

Deconstruction of physician authority brought about broader individual agency for consumers, but also systemic weakness. When pulled off the pedestal, the physician of yore was not replaced by any individual or organized system offering the same level of constancy and commitment.

Healthcare professionals tried to fight the battle, but given that the free market rules of engagement were largely foreign to their professional culture, their efforts backfired, driving wedges into their own professional communities, organized around specialty or institutional identities and entering a zero-sum game, bickering over how dollars are divided among themselves while payers doled them out like parents deciding if they earned their allowance. This fragmentation, pitting provider against provider, only served to weaken the profession even more, with patients losing trust as healthcare professionals were distracted and reduced in their capacity for concern and connection.

In his 1978 book, *Behind the Mirror: the Search for the Natural History of Human Knowledge,* Nobel Prize-winning ethologist Konrad Lorenz described evolution as a process rooted in interaction with, and perception of, the outer world. Drawing from his research, Lorenz describes how organisms and species use exploratory behavior to acquire information necessary to advance their development; he highlights "learning after maturity," in particular, as an important evolutionary advantage.

However, at a fundamental level, healthcare is often unconsciously considered by its members to be a "mature species." While medicine has a deep commitment to clinical innovation — exploring new ideas in terms of our understanding of patients and patient care — there is little exploratory behavior and associated "learning after maturity" for medicine as a profession. It is little wonder then that healthcare is being buffeted by external forces and struggling to make progress on its evolutionary path. And as we know, when the forces of maturity are strong, some species make desperate attempts to resist, resulting in further marginalization from the evolutionary progress.

Since its origins as a profession, medicine has operated under the fee-for-service model: physicians are paid per patient encounter. We took care of the patient and they either paid or they did not; if not, sometimes we took a chicken. However, for most of the history of modern medicine, providers were paid to manage disease, not prevent it, which incentivized them to expand their operations around identifying and managing illness, not improving health. With the dramatic increases in the prevalence of chronic conditions in society over the last thirty years, things looked pretty good for sick care providers.

Until it didn't.

As costs rose, those footing the bill for care began to look at how that money was being spent and identified a number of factors in the sick care system where there was opportunity to set some standards and practices and share some risks. The first wave was something called "managed care."

In the 1990s, the medical community initially viewed the first wave of managed care with interest, engaged around ideas about primary care gatekeepers and evidence-based clinical practice. However, in practice, providers were marginalized as payers inserted themselves to dominate primary relationship management with patients. This model added significant administrative burdens on provider practices and subsequently left the entire medical community with the professional equivalent of post-traumatic stress disorder.

As third-party payers began to manipulate physician fees and increase administrative expenses, the only way to sustain economic stability was to increase the volume of patients cared for in any given day, further disrupting the potential for connection between providers and their patients and forcing providers to practice assembly-line medicine.

You can't walk into Home Depot and name your own price for a refrigerator, but under fee-for-service "managed care," payers regularly reduce and often deny payments even after services have been rendered. This occurs under the guise of a set of rules called "medical necessity," which creates a dangerous adversarial situation that pits the professional judgment of practicing physicians against insurance company determinations. The requirements of documentation required to receive payments, known colloquially as "reimbursement," are burdensome and designed in favor of the payer keeping their cash as long as possible. The term "reimbursement" is a euphemistic acknowledgement of the fact that the provider has already delivered value to the patient and shouldered the economic responsibility for the costs of their staff, supplies, and infrastructure. In some cases, the payers have a conflict of interest due to economic incentives around plan-specific quality measures or goals to reduce overall spending on the "covered lives" of their plan. While there is an appeals process for denials, this further shifts the practice's resources, time, attention, and energy away from patient care. It also shifts the work of worry by providers from their patient's well-being to their own — a dangerous fragmentation of professional focus.

The next evolutionary wave sought to give consumers some control over how their healthcare dollars were spent under the rubric of "consumer directed healthcare." This was operationalized by the insurance companies as high-deductible health plans, presented to the public under the illusion of control but in actuality forced cost-sharing by patients without associated reductions in insurance premiums. This allowed the plans to sustain themselves at the expense of patients. Unfortunately, for many Americans, it seems this strategy had a negative effect on care, with more and more individuals postponing or delaying both necessary and preventive care. This actually increased the risk of patients seeking care only when their conditions were more complex and chronic.

To redirect incentives to some evidence-based preventive services, payers shifted from fee-for-service to fee-for-value, where "value" is contextual and currently grounded in a financial calculus of efficiency, risk-reduction, and managed resource utilization. Value-based payments are either a) embedded in capitated fees, b) tied to utilization-associated metrics and quality measures with known health-economic value, or c) associated with taking full economic risk for patients' care.

While you can draw a dotted line between the standards and quality of care, the "value" of the current models of value-based care accrues first to the "at-risk" entity and second, if at all, to the patient, creating inherent bias in the systems of care that have developed around it. Even the word "risk" has different meanings to health plans and clinicians: when an insurance executive says "risking risk" they are talking about the risk of expense, not the risk of a new diagnosis or the exacerbation of an existing condition.

This trend, known variously as "population health" or "accountable care," shifts the focus from caring for patients who self-select for care to taking transcendent responsibility for the health status of a cohort or population of patients. The initial stimulus for this shift has come under the rubric of a "Triple Aim," defined by Don Berwick and the Institute for Healthcare Improvement.

The Triple Aim was initially imagined as a methodology to improve the performance of systems of care by focusing on three dimensions:

- Improving the patient experience of care (including quality and satisfaction);

- Improving the health of populations;

- Reducing the per capita cost of healthcare.

In recent years, some have added a fourth element related to improving the work life of those who deliver care, creating a Quadruple Aim.

However, whether triple, quadruple, or quintuple, the locus of control for defining value continues to rest with the payers.

Most value-based contracts are based on two factors: first, the achievement, across a defined cohort of patients, of a set of specific metrics of quality with known health-economic value (such as the use of medications that reduce cardiovascular risk in patients with diabetes, or the administration of influenza vaccines in the elderly), and second, a reduction in the unnecessary use of services, such as emergency room utilization or hospitalizations for conditions which could otherwise be treated in the office or clinic. Whether shared savings or full-risk, total-cost of care, the value is defined by economics, not the quality of health of individuals or the attributed population.

*The locus of control for defining value continues to rest with the payers.*

## How Do We Evolve from Here?

Trying to fight a healthcare battle on other people's (largely economic) terms is almost always a losing proposition. Demonstrating that the value of professionals transcends line-item economics will require a shift of the battlefield to one in which professionals — physicians, nurses, and pharmacists, among others — dominate the science of solving human problems.

This will require a truly inclusive professional community rallying around a singularly decisive point: a formal model of collaboration that's achieving results on common goals by sharing responsibility, authority, and accountability, and believing that benefits of collaboration will offset costs associated with loss of autonomy, turf, or even venerable institutions.

*Creating healthcare businesses or new products will not help improve our systems of care until we have the care framework into which they sensibly fit.*

Species with limited genetic variation are less able to adapt to changing environmental conditions; healthcare would benefit considerably if we diversified our professional and conceptual DNA.

This also means that the productive evolution of patient care will not come from a product or technology, nor from any intellectual property, but from evolving our clinical operating model and organizing principles, and the associated doctrines of learning and leadership. Creating healthcare businesses or new products will not help improve our systems of care until we have the care framework into which they sensibly fit.

The "golden age of medicine," whether true or apocryphal, was built on the foundation of knowledge sharing and professional community. Our capacity to improve the quality of care we deliver, and the quality of health achieved by individuals and communities, will only come from wresting control of healthcare's evolution to once again bring wholeness and integrity to the lives of our patients and the communities we serve.

The key to shifting the current evolutionary dynamic in healthcare is an understanding that future healthcare is going to require capabilities and competencies with which the current healthcare community has very limited experience and, in some cases, no real frame of reference. Evolution of our roles and responsibilities is inevitable, and the more we explore the outside world for models and solutions to integrate and adopt as our own, the more likely we are to make magical discoveries and support our own advancement and prosperity as a community and as professionals. Finally, we need to be prepared that there may be some elements of our current state that we cannot protect from the forces of evolution and may have to radically change to prevent extinction.

We are in the *care* business, after all.

Foremost, we must define the goals of our healthcare system: what is the intent and purpose for healthcare in general and the profession of medicine within it? Only then can we determine the requirements for our model of care and its associated systems and define the metrics for investments intended to improve the health of our communities.

# 3

# Achieving Healthcare's Social Imperative: How We Pay, or How We Plan?

HEALTHCARE ECONOMICS — financing, cost control, and payment reform — has dominated our national conversation. These discussions about healthcare in America are fundamentally flawed, because we're more focused on *how we pay* for care than *how we care.*

The focus on economics has been the primary driver of care delivery redesign, especially around the concept of value-based care.

*"Value-based care" is not necessarily driven by values that prevail towards the social imperative.*

However, "value-based care" is not necessarily driven

by values that prevail towards the social imperative; it is currently grounded in a financial calculus of efficiency, risk-reduction, and managed resource utilization. Value-based payments are either embedded in capitated fees or tied to utilization-associated metrics and quality measures with known health-economic value. This focus puts patients and professionals in a subordinate position: despite substantial investments of time, money, and energy, neither the adoption of information technologies nor the expanded access to coverage has demonstrated the value of improved patient outcomes, while both are associated with the unintended consequences of professional dissatisfaction and burnout.

To understand how to prioritize values that prevail toward the social imperative, here are three points.

First, we are overpaying and underserving right now. Instead, we need to develop a new model for investments in the health of our citizens that combines our existing investments in biomedical, behavioral, and social determinants of health into a "whole person" economic model that integrates health, education, fitness, employment, housing, and infrastructure, and supports and prioritizes the capacity of community fixtures and government to sustain the health and well-being of communities.

Second, we need to stop designing the way we deliver care around the way we pay for care. Instead, let's determine, as we have for education, what is an equitable level of care for everyone to get across their lifespan and ensure every American can access that level of care.

Third, we must recognize that, in the short term, we're going to have to invest heavily in undoing the otherwise preventable damage done to our nation by the way we've underserved Americans' health for the last thirty years.

## What's the Purpose of Our Systems of Care?

What if achievement of healthcare's intent and purpose is *not* grounded in economics or technology? What if the traditional organizing principles of medicine are insufficient to allow for the adoption of the kind of problem representations that can support the intent, purpose, and needs of 21st-century systems of care?

If the social imperative of our system of care is to improve quality of health in order to enhance the capacity of individuals to contribute emotionally, socially, and economically as active, productive members of family and community, then we owe the beneficiaries of our system every opportunity to optimize their outcomes, and we owe those funding the system every opportunity to realize the value of their investment. With this as a backdrop, the solution to healthcare's current challenges may be less about how we pay for care and more about how we plan for care.

Despite declarations of commitment to patient-centered care, the fact is that our systems of care remain firmly grounded in the traditional medical model, which is dominated by a focus on diagnoses, condition, medication lists, and testing, and generally excludes functional status, behavioral health, and social determinants from its architecture and organizing principles of care. This is why most efforts to improve the quality of care at the person-level have focused on pre- and post-provider interventions downstream from initial patient engagement: care coordination, care management, coaching, closure of gaps-in-care, home care, remote patient monitoring, social determinants, and others.

There is increasing evidence as to the power of human connection and non-categorical approaches to illness to improve our understanding of a patient's quality of health, as well as to enhance engagement, acceptance, commitment, and behavioral activation to goal-oriented care planning. These insights transcend diagnoses and acknowledge the power of emotion in influencing interactions in relationships.

If we've learned anything from our experience with electronic medical records, it's that we should consider the intent and purpose of the systems we envision before building infrastructure. Imagine what our EMR systems would look like if we had considered how they could enhance our capacity to improve health rather than replicating the artifacts of encounter capture for billing and coding? It's the underlying information architecture, the systemic, structural, and orderly principles to making something work that makes the difference, not just the existence of the platform.

In 1983, Dr. Robert Gordon, special assistant to the director of the NIH, published a critique of the traditional approach of classifying prevention strategies based on origins of disease, proposing a new framework for operational classification of patient-focused clinical strategies. Gordon defined prevention strategies by their predictable outcomes, targeted to those "for whom the measure is advisable on a cost-benefit basis."

Despite these recommendations, medicine still doesn't have an accepted information architecture for care planning; there isn't even a collective definition for the nature of a care plan. Before designing any framework or platforms for universal coverage, perhaps there needs to be a clear understanding of what we expect such coverage to accomplish, and how.

In our current systems, the responsibility for the elements of a patient's care is apportioned independently among a "health resource community," currently defined as the cohort of professionals involved in a patient's care, including but not limited to primary care and specialist physicians, nurses, case managers, therapists, social workers, and others who, based on the mental model of their discipline, contribute insights and related orders or action items.

Unfortunately, even when everyone is at the table (or facing the patient for that matter), collaboration in healthcare is often no more real than the parallel play of toddlers. This aggregation model can result in conflicting priorities in terms of resource allocation, limitations on sharing knowledge and resources, redundancies, miscommunications, clashes in advice and counsel, and potential risks due to conflicts in evidence, especially when judgments are made in isolation of other members of the patient's health resource community.

In reality, an individual's health resource community is much larger, including all those individuals, organizations, entities, and environments (including the patient and their family) that have any involvement, be it actual, virtual, or potential, in managing or influencing variables that have an effect on a patient's health status.

We can increase the scope and power of care as well as better ensure patient-centered success by orchestrating the actions of a patient's health resource community, irrespective of any formal affiliations or lack thereof, and managing the system-level context in which they work. This includes both goal-based and role-based interactions, as well as the interaction design of the resource community itself.

However, as we know from the symphony, orchestration is difficult without a common score that integrates diverse instrumental voices while accounting for their different, but potentially harmonious, roles. Likewise, truly integrated care is impossible without a similar "single source of truth" for a patient's health-related goals and associated plans of care.

A universal care plan architecture would integrate these perspectives and serve as the "single source of truth" for the patient, orchestrating collaboration and accountability across all the members of a patient's health resource community.

An integrated, person-centered architecture for how we plan for care would allow us to more accurately determine the requirements, and value, of investments to improve the health of our citizens and allocate resources to ensure care plan goal achievement. See Appendix 1 for an example as derived from Gordon. Adopting such an operating framework would ensure that every member of society has the same opportunity to optimize their health status, while accounting for both individualized person-level goals and the system-level (USPHS, HEDIS, ACO measures) goals imposed or required by third parties.

## *The Plan for Care*

A universal architecture for how we plan for care and allocate resources to ensure care plan goal achievement would allow us to determine the requirements and value of investments to improve the health of our citizens. Such an architecture would:

a. Orient all the members of a patient's health resource-community toward the whole person;

b. Account for all the possible system- and person-level goals necessary to improve or sustain a patient's quality of health, including lifestyle/wellness, selected and indicated prevention, risk and condition management, and palliation;

c. Eliminate artificial boundaries related to the biopsychosocial determinants (molecular, physiological, structural, neuropsychological, environmental, genomic, biomic, or social) of a patient's conditions or risks;

d. Integrate and account for acute, chronic, preventive, functional, and spiritual conditions.

Drawing on robust mathematical models that support optimized decision-making in the presence of uncertainty, such a framework would also require a shift in the focus on diagnosis as the basis of decision-making to a more precise understanding and description of a patient's condition in terms of their current state relative to their health-related goals. Under this model, "condition" will be defined by three key state-related variables that are often referred to but are rarely operationalized in medical care:

- **Physical state: primary observable, tangible variables**

- **Informational state: secondary or derived knowledge about a state**

- **Belief state: the perspective of the agent under observation about their state**

Two patients with the same symptoms or diagnoses may have very different conditions. This new clinical vocabulary will be used to better describe conditions in terms of state-related variables and, as such, better shape the strategies-to-goal for care.

The purpose of a care plan is then grounded in the strategies and resources required to effect change from "current state" to "goal-state." This is accomplished by monitoring the state of the patient's risks and conditions, and escalating and de-escalating clinical and other resources to effect productive changes in the patient's health status and/or associated molecular, physiological, structural, neuropsychological, environmental, genomic, biomic, or social benchmarks (see Appendix 2). In the case of diagnostic processes, it would involve orchestrating an optimized scope and sequence by which state-related variables are identified and categorized.

The adoption and integration of a universal integrated care plan framework would ensure that every member of society has the same opportunity to optimize their health status, enhance the capacity of a patient's entire health resource community to monitor and contribute to progress towards goals, and allow for a rational and individualized approach to intervention design and resource allocation towards healthcare's social imperative while assuring a concordant, harmonious experience for the patient.

# 4

# Unconscious Bias in Healthcare System Strategies Leaves Patients Second

WITH THE POOREST urban congressional district in the United States, the Bronx has long been held as representative of the challenges and consequences of health inequities. It should then come as no surprise that the Bronx had been especially hard hit by COVID-19 since, for the last seven years in a row, it has been deemed New York state's "unhealthiest" county in the annual countyhealthrankings.com list, published by the University of Wisconsin Population Health Institute and the Robert Wood Johnson Foundation (RWJF).

However, the Bronx is far from underserved: there are 9-plus advanced teaching hospitals, an internationally renowned medical school, and more than 4,000 physicians who work within its 42 square miles (and that's not counting all the nurses, pharmacists, therapists, and social workers). That's one provider for every 350 of its 1,400,000 people; almost 100 physicians per capita for every square mile. With all that clinical firepower, you'd think we could do better; yet the Bronx has remained vulnerable and unhealthy.

The same is true for Pittsburgh, where a 2019 report on gender and race inequality found that Pittsburgh's rate of infant mortality for Black babies is more than six times higher than it is for white babies, and people of color have a higher prevalence of cardiovascular disease, cancers, and a host of other adverse outcomes, including premature mortality. Yet Pittsburgh is far from underserved; between the two major health systems, UPMC and Allegheny (which together generate more than $25 billion in revenue), there are over 48 hospitals in the region and more than 7,000 employed physicians. While many of those physicians may be hospital-based specialists, it is enough for one doctor for every 400 of the 3,000,000 people in the 28-county Pittsburgh megaregion, and one for every 250 people in the five-county region surrounding Pittsburgh proper.

There is ample evidence that health status of a population affects economic vitality directly through enhanced labor productivity and reduced burden of illness on individuals and families, but also indirectly through the impact that health has on educational opportunity. If this is the value of a healthy community, what's kept the Bronx's last place streak going for seven years?

Despite their long-standing commitments and contributions to community health improvement initiatives (UPMC cites $1.4 billion in 'IRS-defined community benefit' *What's kept the Bronx's last place streak going for seven years?*

for 2019), the fact is that large health systems, which often control a significant amount of care delivery in disadvantaged communities, have an existential conflict between the needs of the community and the needs of the institution. Organizations like the Bronx-based Montefiore Medical Center and its affiliated medical school generate a proportion of their $6.2 billion in annual revenue and research funding from the economic value of preventable illness and vulnerability of the community. The 'value' of that investment should be defined and judged by the community itself, not an IRS-regulation. Are we unintentionally shaping our investments in the health of hospitals over the health of their service areas?

## Upstream Failures

In engineering, a fail-safe is a downstream feature of a system that is designed to minimize harm associated with some form of upstream system failure. Fire-sensitive sprinkler systems are a good example; while our primary goal is to prevent fires from occurring in the first place, the sprinklers are there to mitigate the consequences of a failure of fire prevention efforts.

Unfortunately, our healthcare system is designed around the fail-safe model. As a nation we are weak at improving health, but excellent at managing our own upstream failures, as evidenced in the remarkable response of our systems of care to our nation's inability to contain COVID-19; treating sick people remains a very valuable thing to do, so there is little incentive to organize our systems of care beyond biomedical or biomechanical interventions.

*Treating sick people remains a very valuable thing to do, so there is little incentive to organize our systems of care beyond biomedical or biomechanical interventions.*

The biggest barriers to improving the quality of health of communities like the Bronx are the continued dominance of the fail-safe biomedical model and the economic basis by which healthcare is valued. This introduces unconscious bias into organizational decision-making: people need to be sick for most healthcare organizations to be successful; a truly healthy community could threaten their existence.

Even recent interest in the social determinants of health is driven by economic incentives associated with managing utilization of hospital-based services by individual patients, not the upstream socioeconomic and educational inequities and systemic racism that are the root cause of those determinants and undermine the vitality and health of our communities. Building an addition on the house of medicine does not change its foundation.

Instead of access to care, perhaps it is time to consider quality of health as the social imperative of our systems of care, focusing on the value of health to support and improve the capacity of individuals to succeed in the world on their own terms and contribute as active, productive members of family and community. This would become the basis by which we determine the requirements for our model of care and its associated systems and define the metrics for return on investments intended to improve the health of our citizens.

## Genuine Collaboration

Most of the tens of billions of dollars spent on medical care for the citizens of the Bronx, and communities like it, come from government — city, state, and federal — coffers, but are parsed among many dozens of institutions such as hospitals and health systems, managed care plans, community health centers, and group practices that traditionally operate under a respectful compact of mutual self-interest, but do not genuinely collaborate.

There is no formal model for collaboration — a form of interaction design — as a healthcare discipline; an operational framework, with benchmarks for performance and accountability, will be required for us to achieve the social imperative. Upstream transformation towards a tangible improvement in the quality of health of individuals and communities will only work if all share the belief that the benefits of collaboration will offset the loss of autonomy, "turf," or even some venerable institutions.

*An operational framework, with benchmarks for performance and accountability, will be required for us to achieve the social imperative.*

Genuine collaboration will require government to shift from their existing, fragmented, investments to a 'whole-person/whole-community' economic model, and require orchestration of health, educational, and social services resources towards community-level goal achievement, where objective measures of health status — such as the RWJF County

Health Rankings or Pittsburgh's Index of Ranked Livability — are the gauges of success and payment.

Under the social imperative the traditional biomedical perspective will become subordinate to a person-centered definition of health, driving new, non-categorical approaches to how we assess and intervene to improve the health of individuals and communities. However, we also need to be aware that the same unconscious bias that drives institutional self-preservation will provoke desperate attempts to resist change and preserve current institutional structures. The fact is that if we are successful in our social imperative for health, many of our current institutions, resources, and roles may become superfluous.

It's time to organize our resources towards a collective leadership strategy to protect, and improve, the health and well-being of the multicultural Bronx and similar communities around the country. With full recognition of the acute and intensive care challenges facing hospitals and health systems otherwise avoidable downstream pathology, all it would take is a conscious decision on the part of healthcare stakeholders and influencers — professional communities, business leaders, government, and civil society — to shift their focus to supporting collective accountability as the basis of the road map and incentives for geographic population health, and finally address the persistent barriers to achieving the social imperative in communities disadvantaged by economic and social inequities. Let's stop the parallel play and come together to put people and community first.

# 5

# Diagnosis Doesn't Matter

THERE'S A SAYING in the autism community: "If you've met one person with autism, you've met one person with autism." While obviously a reference to phenotypic neurodiversity and the need to judge people as individuals, there's an underlying construct here that can inform our efforts to realize the social imperative of health: there's a difference between someone's *diagnosis*, their *condition*, and their *problem*. In medicine, we tend to conflate these concepts: our "problem lists" or "condition lists" are really just a list of diagnoses, and not a reflection of the patient's current state nor their aspirational or optimal state. Autism may be a diagnosis, but it gives no indication of the individual's condition, as might be indicated by their functional

> *There's a difference between someone's diagnosis, their condition, and their problem.*

status or level of personal adjustment, nor is every individual with autism burdened by the problems associated with autism-related disabilities. The same framework can be applied to any common chronic condition: diabetes, congestive heart failure, chronic obstructive pulmonary disease, multiple sclerosis, or the consequences of events such as stroke or traumatic brain injury.

Medicine has made synonyms of the terms diagnosis, problem, and condition. These are not just semantic differences; it is well established that the organizing principles of knowledge can have a profound effect on the capacity to define and solve problems. Our lack of clarity on the relationships between these concepts may, in fact, be a major barrier to our capacity to design effective care. The biomedical model introduces unconscious bias that may limit the development of problem representations that incorporate the necessary complexity and context to support adequate person-centered solution development.

## What is the Problem?

The reality is there are three distinct elements of an information architecture that can support more effective efforts to improve quality of health.

| Diagnosis | The presence of physical material or information that meets diagnostic criteria or is associated with disease-specific pathology. |
|---|---|
| Condition | The current state of the individual with a specific diagnosis. |
| Problem | A discrepancy between an individual's current state and an aspirational or optimal state; a risk of instability of their current condition; risk factors for acquiring a diagnosis, change in functional status, or burden associated with quality of health. |

This reality requires us to adopt a new framework for describing the conditions associated with a patient's diagnosis and defining their problems in terms of that condition relative to goals for their health, whether based on shared decision-making, system-determined, or what is urgent/emergent. Under this framework, the ICD Classification System — initially designed as a controlled vocabulary for international epidemiologic reporting — no longer holds up as clinically relevant and, except in research settings, becomes an unnecessarily complex administrative burden to providing care, as it does not support the clinical operating model.

Having a diagnosis is not itself a problem, unless its condition (current state) is undesirable or unsatisfying (via symptoms, distress, functional capacity or disability, risks, or prognosis). In addition, while etiology may be the determinant of a diagnosis, it may, or may not, be a determinant of the patient's condition.

Without a precise understanding and description of a patient's condition (their current state relative to a diagnosis), we cannot determine the true nature of their problem, nor its appropriate solution. Perhaps a reconsideration of our clinical vocabulary and taxonomy of care planning is required if we are going to effectively operationalize our capacity to improve or sustain the quality of health of individuals and communities. The first step is to stop using diagnosis as the foundation of our plans of care.

*The first step is to stop using diagnosis as the foundation of our plans of care.*

One challenge we face in the productive evolution of our system of care is operationalizing our information architecture beyond the diagnosis-treatment binary, and finding ways to define and describe:

1. The patient's condition (their current state)

2. The aspired to, or optimal, state

3. The problem model that defines the goals for the patient and any related strategies for care or intervention

Understanding the patient's current condition, as defined by the status of state-dependent variables, and compared to benchmarks of an optimal state, will dramatically increase our capacity to effect positive and productive change in people's lives.

## *Condition*

The World Health Organization defines health as a "state of complete physical, mental and social well-being and not merely the absence of disease or infirmity."

Under the social imperative, "quality of health" transcends specific diagnoses, because it is a reflection of the extent to which those diagnoses (as well as other determinants) affect the individual's capacity to contribute — emotionally, socially, and economically — as active, productive members of family and community. Treating diagnoses as discrete elements is necessary but insufficient to achieve the social imperative; understanding how those diagnoses (and other factors) affect their capacity to contribute becomes the operative model for patient assessment.

*There is value to the community and society-at-large to prevent otherwise avoidable suffering, morbidity, and disability.*

In this case, the word "contribute" means to help to cause or bring about, or to participate in the achievement or provision of something. It does not presume any specific value systems or political orientation as to the nature of the contribution; it may be purely personal and individual, or involve the lives of others. The social imperative only presumes that there is value to the community and society-at-large to prevent otherwise avoidable suffering, morbidity, and disability, and support all citizens to succeed in the world on their own terms.

Within this framework, it is not a diagnosis itself, but the extent to which the patient's diagnoses — and other determinants — are influencing or shaping their:

- **Functional status**
- **Personal adjustment**
- **Coping capacity**
- **Spiritual and personal development**

Between 1982 and 1992, Drs. Ruth Stein and Dorothy Jessop of the Albert Einstein College of Medicine in the Bronx conducted a series of elegant studies defining and exploring "a non-categorical approach" to chronic illness. Their insights into the transcendent functional burden of illness, independent of diagnostic labels or etiology, provides a currently unrealized opportunity for assessment and intervention design.

Independently, Dr. Robert Gordon, special assistant to the director of the NIH, published a critique of the traditional approach of classifying prevention strategies based on 'origins of disease,' proposing a new framework for "operational classification" of patient-focused clinical strategies. Gordon defined prevention strategies by the predictable outcomes of those measures targeted to "those persons not currently feeling the effects of a disease, intended to decrease the risk that that disease will afflict them in the future."

This approach to understanding an individual's quality of health is supported by a twenty-five-year-plus body of research on the disproportionately adverse effects of "allostatic load" on health status.

Allostatic load is a non-categorical indicator of health and refers to the demands and burdens on the body and brain related to repeated biopsychosocial challenges and adverse social, economic, and physical environments. Factors influencing allostatic load include genomics, race and ethnicity, early life experiences, emotional climate, lifestyle, learned behaviors, locus of control, socioeconomic status, social relationships, and resilience.

Allostatic load can be measured and has been associated with deteriorating health, illness burden, early mortality, poor pregnancy outcomes, maternal mortality, and disability; it has provided unique insights into the health status of low-income, disadvantaged, and racial minority communities and is a unique framework for systems of care that may overcome systemic bias.

## *Problem Modeling*

Health-related decision-making is fundamentally an optimization function in the face of uncertainty (given the extreme variation in the human condition); and it starts with an understanding of the variables that are determinants of the current condition. Filtered through the perspective of Warren Powell, a professor of operations research at Princeton University who researches optimization decision-making in the face of uncertainty, "condition" can be understood as the calculus of three sets of variables:

### 1. Physical Variables

The measurable elements of tangible systems, resources or environments; physical variables can account for molecular, physiological, structural, biomic, and environmental determinants. These can be described in a number of forms:

- o Scalar (an elemental unit indicating some level of relative or contextual magnitude; e.g., Hemoglobin A1C level; pollen count);

- o Vector (reflecting both magnitude and direction; e.g., Myocardial infarction; housing conditions);

- ○ Matrices (a relational framework for variables; e.g., Metastatic cancer; access to healthcare); or

- ○ Tensors (a dynamic multidimensional array in which the organizing entity interacts with and transforms the other entities in the structure; e.g., Sepsis with multiorgan system failure; poverty).

## 2. Informational Variables

Known parameters that can affect or influence the condition and can add value or insight to model a situation, compute a transition probability, determine an objective function (the best element from the set of available alternatives), or make a decision. Informational variables include but are not limited to genomic, biomic, or social elements.

## 3. Belief Variables

Probabilistic information about unknown or unobservable parameters, or uncertainties that can affect or influence the condition; predictions based on prior experience; neuropsychological factors; spiritual, cultural or faith-based beliefs, independent of evidence or other informational variables.

## *What Does Matter?*

How someone feels. Sadly, the word "feeling" means one thing when patients talk to family and friends, and something completely different — and inhumanely narrow — when patients speak to healthcare professionals. When a healthcare professional asks a patient, "How do you feel?", patients unconsciously know they are referring to physical symptoms. When your parent or aunt or best friend asks you the same questions, they want to know your emotional and spiritual state. It's only when emotions are overwhelming — potentially pathological — do they cross the line to meet the medical criteria for 'feelings.'

This is not to deny that the burden of illness is an important factor in an individual's health, but medicine does not even have a vocabulary to assess or document the burden of illness independent of physical symptoms or pathology of an existence of a specific diagnosis.

So what is health? How do we determine the goals for a patient's future state?

You ask them. Explore their life purpose, their level and aspirations for personal productivity, and their social and community engagement. Then examine their current state — conditions and their determinants — through this filter. This becomes the basis of the "person-level goals" in their care plan.

The World Health Organization itself provides us a powerful alternative to the sick care ICD-10 codes for disease: their International Classification of Function (ICF). While initially developed as a standard language for disability, its utility is transcendent as a general classification system that:

> "provide(s) a scientific basis for understanding and studying health and health-related states,

*outcomes, determinants, and changes in health status and functioning, (while) establish(ing) a common language for describing health and health-related states...(and) permit(ting) comparison of data across countries, healthcare disciplines, services and time; and provide(ing) a systematic coding scheme for health information systems."*

The ICF has been earnestly applied and tested in pediatrics, where the ICF framework has been humorously reimagined as the "F-words" to support the care of children with disability: function, family, fitness, fun, friends, and future. This taxonomy becomes a way to clinically operationalize ICF for care planning and shared decision-making with patients.

## *Intervention: Strategies and Tactics*

Once there is an understanding of the patient's condition, current state goals for health, and what matters to them for their future state, interventions can be crafted. Healthcare interventions generally seek to a) attenuate any risks to their aspirational or optimal state, b) reduce any burdens associated with acute or chronic conditions, and c) seek to sustain or improve functional and spiritual state.

Interventions are built in two stages: the first stage is the development of a strategic framework, and the second is the tactical plan to make the framework real.

A strategy is a conceptual framework, directional and its elements actionable; it is the framework to show how we will go from *what is* to *what should be*; for any intervention there can be multiple strategies. Meanwhile, the tactical plan focuses on which resources should be mustered or deployed to realize the strategy; then how they should be integrated and orchestrated in order to achieve maximum effect and efficiency. Health systems designed to achieve the social imperative require tactical capabilities and competencies at all levels of the hierarchy.

As noted before, there are often other goals — community or population-level — that the systems of care aspire to achieve for everyone (like seatbelt use or dental care), or specific cohorts of patients (e.g., all diabetics). These arise from policies — rules or functions that determine a decision given the available information in the current state of the system under investigation. While these system-level policies may be desirable based on objective evidence, if they do not organically arise during person-level goal setting, they should be managed, and prioritized, with the patient under a shared decision-making model. The fact is that there should be no imposition of goals on the patient; if they are contextually relevant to the patient's quality of health, it is our job to educate, activate, and motivate patients to accept and commit to them.

# 6

# Making Beautiful Music Together

IMAGINE YOUR JOB was to work with a small team of people to solve the same eight problems every day. Pretty easy, right? It might even bore you after a while.

However, just because the problems are the same every day does not mean that every day is the same. People are different every day; moods and attitudes change, distractions occur. These factors might just affect the performance of the team, its consistency, efficiency, and outcomes.

Now imagine that you have to solve these problems for a different group of people every day, and your compensation was based not just on your technical performance, but on the degree of affinity you were able to achieve with them.

So, in addition to managing the variability in the performance capacity of the team, you also had to manage the individual experience of the person(s) judging your performance—your capacity to create an immersive, transformative experience for them in real-time.

Such is the life of the musician, for it is the consistency of both their performance and the depth of connection with the listener that drives the value of their concert tickets and recordings.

Like musical performance, managing health and the associated delivery of healthcare is a time-space activity in that it is temporally linear and dimensional in experience; it only exists when being performed.

The delivery of healthcare is grounded in the model of solo performance — physician-patient; nurse-patient; therapist-patient — where performance parameters are largely based on technical attributes of the provider, often operating independently of other members of the patient's health resource-community. This is both derived from and sustained by the models of education and training of healthcare professionals, and is unconsciously embedded in the organizational attributes and processes of healthcare delivery.

Further, the operating model for care delivery and the management of systems of practice is derived from the *command-and-control* model, where a designated authority provides direction over subordinate resources. Traditionally, physicians constituted the dominant authority over other disciplines, while modern operating models in other "mission-critical" industries — such as telecommunications, defense, or mass transit — with high expectations for performance have evolved into more collaborative shared-command structures.

Efforts to improve or sustain quality of health involve the production of complex sequences and span different modalities and dimensions. As such, achievement of the social imperative will require a higher level of coordination and mastery of collaborative group performance practices in order to achieve the expressive intent of actions intended to improve quality of health of individuals and communities; an ensemble approach to care delivery.

## *Ensemble Thinking*

Collaboration is not a formal discipline in healthcare, and the healthcare ecosystem does not have a transdisciplinary operating model for collaboration. Each discipline — medicine nursing, pharmacy, psychology — presumes authority in its realm, but the patients experience is disharmonious, undermining their trust in the system; conflicts abound, with little opportunity for, or process of, adjudication.

Our capacity to achieve the social imperative is undermined when members of an individual's health resource-community think their role transcends the collaborative, and their opinions transcend the data. They become like members of an orchestra who never play unless it is their solo, otherwise standing around talking on their cell phones and crumpling food wrappers while the rest of the orchestra is working hard to perform seamlessly off the same score.

Under the ensemble model of healthcare, quality will be determined by the extent to which the different roles and perspectives that constitute an individual's health resource-community are able to interweave their linear succession of time-space events into a single experiential entity.

This does not mean everyone is playing the same thing at the same time. In fact, successful care delivery will require the opposite: multiple melody lines, sometimes in simultaneous consonance — harmony — and sometimes with one player in the foreground but supported by background accompaniment.

Ensemble thinking eradicates dominant-subordinate relationships and dissolves the realms that serve as self-protective niches for professional disciplines, while supporting the masterful performance of technical and interpretive experts, each of whom has invested years in mastering their specific instrument or craft, coming together, subsuming their individual identities and, in a shared effort, creating a concordant, goal-directed experience and to move people in ways that are quite powerful.

In the ensemble, performers use their instruments to express their part of a score (individually and in concert), to create a harmonious experience for the audience. In healthcare, the score is represented by their *plan of care* — the mutually agreed upon aspirational or optimal goals for their quality of health. However, as the best musicians know, despite the score being the same, a composition is never played the same way twice. Performers use their instruments in collective effort to create a harmonious and moving experience for the audience, and can transcend the score by being mindful of the emotional content of the piece, the audience, and each other, because the performance only exists in the collective experience.

Ensemble thinking creates a community of equals, serves as an organizing framework for their focus on the audience (individual or group), and provides a set of rules for their interactions in service of the transformational effect they are seeking to produce.

The delivery of care must be viewed as a performance: a bi-directional energy exchange with the patient and within and among the patient's health-resource ensemble. The nature of human performance that generates transformative change has been studied

*The delivery of care must be viewed as a performance: a bi-directional energy exchange with the patient and within and among the patient's health-resource ensemble.*

in detail by, among others, researchers such as Klaus Scherer at the Swiss Center for Affective Sciences, Marcel Zentner at the University of Innsbruck, and John Solboda at the GuildHall School in the UK. Their research has identified the input variables associated with the transformational power of musical performance. These studies identify how elements of performance contribute to emotional states, using regression analysis to understand the 'factor power' of specific elements and how they operate in concert (additive vs. multiplicative; linear vs. non-linear). These studies have parallels in research on the role of syntax and perception of expressive speech. Performance elements are demonstrated to convey information and energy via both iconic and symbolic coding.

Typically, in healthcare, only three factors are considered as having major influence on outcomes: the patient's current state, any condition-related etiological factors, and the skills and technique of the provider.

However, taken together, this body of research provides direction for a very clear model for the competencies associated with systems of care designed to affect the transformational goals associated with the social imperative. They also help identify current gaps in the education and training of healthcare professionals, the operating capabilities of the systems in which they work, and, most important, new measures of the quality of care that are directly associated with person-centered outcomes.

Adapted from Scherer, the "Transformative Potential" for a healthcare experience can be defined as follows:

---

## Transformative Potential (TP) = PatF x SF x PerF x CF

*KEY: PatF = Patient Features; SF = Structural Features; PerF = Performance Features; CF = Contextual Features*

---

## Patient Features

*Physical State x Informational State x Belief State x Impactability*

Patient features reflect their current 'condition' and their capacity for change.

## Structural Features

*Pace x Tone x Intensity x Theme*

Structural features reflect the nature of the experience and are rarely considered as quality or performance indicators in today's systems of care. However, as in music and other structured experiences, themes can be identified: structural patterns with distinct ordering of characteristics; or the rate, character, and vigor. In healthcare, these would be recognition of thematic patterns associated with common conditions or patient experiences.

## Performance Features

*Presence x Technique x Accuracy x Consonance*

Performance features refer to the way the experience is implemented or managed by members of the individual's health-resource community and have a major impact on the acceptance and commitment to actions necessary to achieve the goals for quality of health. Physical and psychological presence, precision, and sense of concordance associated with collaboration all have effects on individual and collective outcomes.

## Contextual Features

*Circumstances × Frame*

Contextual features refer to both environmental and situational factors, as well as the systems-level and interpersonal relational frameworks in which care is required or delivered.

# Using the formula for Transformative Potential, we can identify a set of primary skills associated with masterful ensemble performance:

| | |
|---|---|
| **Technique** | This reflects the extent to which a professional has mastered their instrument; it includes the timbre, or quality of tone in performance. |
| **Repertoire** | The stock of skills, aptitudes, and capabilities brought to performance, inclusive of, but not exclusive to, technique; this includes skills at co-performance, role recognition, blending, synchronization, cue recognition, response to changes, and improvisation. |
| **Mode** | In music, characteristic patterns of melody constitute a mode; in narrative, a mode is a voice or point of view used to create a narrative. Modes in healthcare can reflect the perspective of the performer (the mode of pediatrics is different that the mode of orthopedic surgery), or can reflect system-level thematic narratives or commonly ordered experiences (acute illness vs chronic illness exacerbation). |
| **Accuracy** | The degree to which your technique and repertoire come together to achieve an outcome. |
| **Dynamics** | How the expressive elements of performance are organized into meaningful combinations, shaped by intent, structure, and arrangement, including duration, substitution, modification, and movement. |
| **Communication** | Listening skills; the capacity to give and receive cues to the patient, their family, caregivers, and those within and among the ensemble. |
| **Emotion** | Expression and acknowledgement of feelings associated with the process of care and associated relationships; the capacity to connect with others beyond the technical requirements of the performance; support to find meaning and value in the experience. |

Imagine now that graduation from medical school and subsequent board certification involves evaluation of your performance in each of these seven areas, not just your factual knowledge or technical skill.

## Ensemble Performance

The work of Peter Keller at the interdisciplinary MARCS Institute for Brain, Behaviour and Development of Western Sydney University in Australia provides a most detailed road map for the development of an ensemble approach to healthcare delivery. The absolute foundation of ensemble performance is shared intent: a unified view of the ideal outcome for a patient. From this shared intent, ensemble members coordinate their actions with both precision and flexibility in order to produce a coherent and transformative experience for the patient.

Keller defines three key elements that must act in concert as the basis of successful ensemble performance achievement:

1. **Anticipatory imagery**

2. **Prioritized integrative attention**

3. **Adaptive timing**

## 1.  Anticipatory Imagery

Ensemble performance requires each member to anticipate and imagine both their performance and the performance of others. This creates a mental representation of the whole and how each member's performance contributes to the shared intent and outcome for the patient. This facilitates the accurate performance of individual parts by priming cognitive, emotive, and motor pathways, anticipating potential conflicts, and enabling action pre-planning.

## 2.  Prioritized Integrative Attention

Joint action as related to efforts to improve quality of health of individuals can be complicated; members of a health resource-community are not only responsible for their parts but also must maintain awareness of the relationship between their parts and the parts performed by others. As such, Keller has demonstrated that successful ensemble performance requires a level of "prioritized integrative attention," a form of joint attention that "involves concurrently paying attention to one's own actions (high priority) and those of others (lower priority) while monitoring the overall ensemble performance." This attentional strategy is assumed to facilitate ensemble cohesion by allowing performers to adjust their actions based on the real-time comparison of mental representations of the performance goal. Performers are thus able to deal with changes in the momentary demands of their own parts and the relationship between their own and others' parts in terms of timing, intensity, intonation, and dynamics.

### 3. Adaptive Timing

The most fundamental requirement of ensemble performance is the coordination of one's own actions with those of others. This requires continuous and consistent adjustment of actions to maintain synchrony in the face of deviations and other — often unpredictable — events. Adaptive skills enable ensemble performers to react to intentions and unintentional variations in each other's performance, as well as the response of the patient.

## *Composition, Interpretation, Improvisation*

In music, composition refers to a work that is designed before performance; generally, a structured, skill-oriented sequence of events (notes, rests) with a pre-determined resolution. In healthcare, composition begins with guidelines and evidence that will shape the performance of members of the ensemble. As diverse roles in the healthcare ensemble may bring different instruments and modes to the performance, the challenge is to orchestrate their performances — and mental models for care — into a single, coherent, goal-directed performance. Performing composed work is based on respect for the text, but also requires some level of interpretation based on the context, the audience, and the moment in which it is being performed.

However, in healthcare, we know things are not always predictable; under these circumstances some level of improvisation needs to take place. In music, improvisation generally refers to spontaneous composition that occurs in performance; this can be part of the planned structure of performance (as in jazz) or based on the need to react to unplanned or spontaneous events. In healthcare, improvisation is goal-achievement by exploration based on technical mastery and historical experience, evaluating progress against some specific criteria.

Unlike composition, interpretation and improvisation take place in real-time and require the ensemble to have some shared conventions of governance — organization, administration, repertoire choices, and mental representations.

## Leadership

Ensemble leadership can be a collective experience when the players listen for change and lead based on need, or — in the case of large ensembles, like the orchestra — via a conductor. However, the conductor is not the leader but serves an essential integrating role, holding the vision for the performance as a whole. Even the most virtuoso players understand they cannot conduct *and* sit first chair; they respect, trust, and defer to the conductor and listen carefully — not for reaction, but for connection — to their peers, because they understand that a solo may be in their hands, but the symphony only exists in the collective effort.

In groups without a formal leadership structure, members of the ensemble may step up at different times to help the whole ensemble navigate certain passages, or to perform in the foreground accompanied by their co-performers. This lead may change based on the structural performance or contextual features.

Although a group may have a leader, or may temporarily highlight an individual's performance, everyone in the group is contributing to the decision-making and creative process. Other dynamics are required for such a group to function effectively: compromise, consensus, subtle influence, respect, openness, or perhaps even calculated assertiveness.

## *Context-Specific Factors*

Ensemble performance places exceptional demands on the mental and physical capabilities of co-performers, and is characterized by the balance between temporal precision and flexibility in role-based coordination. The successful execution of shared goals and plans during ensemble performance is based on the capacity of co-performers to anticipate, attend, and adapt to each other's actions in real-time. The successful application of ensemble strategies and skills is obviously constrained by knowledge of the structure of the condition being addressed and familiarity with the expressive intentions and stylistic tendencies of co-performers. These two varieties of knowledge — structural and personal — serve different functions and different levels of skills and experience and can have dissociable effects on ensemble coordination.

# 7

# Healthcare as a Human Experience

When you think of healthcare, you don't think of systems that engage, inform, motivate, or inspire. Unfortunately, most people go through healthcare events overwhelmed with doubt and confusion. Medicine has traditionally been referred to as a balance of art — skills and craftsmanship — and science. However, recent advances in information technologies have tipped the scales towards data and analytics.

I am sorry to have to be the messenger on this one, but it is time that an important truth be told: you can't find meaning in data. Data may offer you perspective, insights, trends, or viewpoints, but in and of itself, it cannot provide meaning. No matter how much you have and how many different ways you can mathematically analyze it, data by itself is meaningless.

You can, however, find meaning in life, and sometimes data can help you do so.

HEALTHCARE AS A HUMAN EXPERIENCE

In his extraordinary book, *Man's Search for Meaning*, Austrian psychiatrist and Holocaust survivor Viktor Frankl examined what the gruesome experience of Auschwitz and three other Nazi concentration camps taught him about how the quest for meaning, as a primary purpose in life, could sustain, and even influence survival for, those under even the most horrific circumstances.

Frankl's basic premise was that our primary drive in life is not pleasure, but the discovery and pursuit of what we personally find meaningful. While this may be controversial when put in the context of other psychological frameworks for mental health, the evidence supports its power as a driver of health and health-related behavior for both patients and health professionals.

> We can't find meaning in data, but we can find meaning in each other.

For Frankl, meaning came from three possible sources: purposeful work, love, and courage in the face of difficulty.

And for healthcare, meaning comes from people: helping people, caring for people, and dedicating ourselves to others. We can't find meaning in data, but we can find meaning in each other.

You cannot change someone's health status with technology. Caring, compassion, and connection are the dependent foundations for improving both quality of care and quality of health. While the clinician-patient relationship remains the foundation and energizing principle for most healthcare interactions, the fact is that for most people, the decision to commit to a plan of care is based on motivating factors in their lived experience: family, friends, community, and personal objectives.

Since the capacity to improve quality of health is fundamentally a human endeavor, the productive evolution of our systems of care must reward the value of human connection and commitment. Healthcare outcomes dramatically improve when systems of care engage, inform, motivate, and inspire action and connection between patients and their *health-resource community:* those individuals, organizations, entities, and environments that have any involvement — actual, virtual, or potential — to manage or influence variables that have an effect on a patient's health status.

Additional support for this perspective can be found in the work of University of California, Berkeley psychology professor Dr. Dacher Kelter, an expert in the social functions of emotion. His research has dramatic implications for the efficacy of efforts to improve quality of health (it also served as the basis of Pixar's 2015 blockbuster, *Inside Out*).

Kelter's research clearly illustrates how emotions influence interactions in relationships:

- How they help individuals recognize the beliefs and intentions of others

- How they evoke complementary and reciprocal emotions

- How they serve as incentives or deterrents for another individual's behavior

These act as the foundation for the levels of engagement, motivation, aspiration, acceptance, and commitment required to achieve ambitious goals regarding the health status of individuals and populations. Knowing this, there are three key elements of 'experience of care' that need to be incorporated into our clinical operating model for the social imperative:

- An understanding of the factors affecting an individual's capacity for engagement, connection, commitment, and action;

- Aspirational care planning that integrates and reflects their interests, priorities, wishes, goals, and dreams (person-level goals), as well as evidence-based best practices (system-level goals);

- Putting the locus of control for health-related decisions in the hands of the person.

Approaching care planning this way allows us to more accurately determine the requirements and value of investments to improve the health of any specific population.

## *Clinical Outcomes Require Both Style and Substance*

In healthcare right now, experience management mostly refers to customer service and hospitality. But if healthcare is going to meaningfully improve patient outcomes and support staff while responsibly managing finances, systems of care are going to require new perspectives on how to address the needs of patients and members of their care teams.

The success of whole-person care is dependent on the depth of the relationships that arise from the experience of the person eligible for care; these relationships include, but are not limited to, the healthcare and other professionals in the patient's health-resource community. One of the core principles of whole-person care is to empower and enable individuals and their family, friends, and community fixtures to independently support care plan goal achievement.

In healthcare, the factors by which patients judge relationships and quality are less about objective clinical factors than the *tactile* and *emotive* performance of those involved in their care.

- **Tactile Performance**
  - ○ Efficiency, simplicity, consistency, availability, reliability, responsiveness
- **Emotive Performance**
  - ○ Integrity, sincerity, urgency, empathy, dignity, trust, authenticity

Based on the power of tactile and emotive performance to shape behavior, systems to deliver whole-person care are rooted in the principles of socio-technical systems design (STSD). STSD is an approach to design which integrates human, social, and organizational factors, as well as technical factors, into the design of our systems of care. It is a person-first methodology to make interactions with complex systems more efficient, effective, pleasant, or meaningful. A person-first view *acknowledges the influence of emotion, behavioral beliefs, and cognitive load on both patients and staff, and incorporates that understanding into the operating model for care.*

The use of STSD has been perfected in industries that are able to use a combination of sophisticated technologies and human services to build deep connections and trust with their audiences, despite complex large-scale operations that must deliver value while safely serving thousands of diverse audiences daily, such as theme parks, museums, and cultural attractions.

Like healthcare, these industries depend heavily on quality, operational performance, infrastructure, and logistics for their success, but they also put equal discipline into managing the human experience in order to engage, inform, motivate, and inspire action, and create immersive, often transformative, experiences. These industries use design to blur the boundary between performance and audience in order to fully immerse the audience or guests in the direction, scope, and sequence of their journey.

Theme parks, museums, and cultural attractions share many of the demands on healthcare to manage relational and logistic interactions, organizational capacity, quality and safety, human resources, and workforce readiness. But the true foundation of their success is their powerful capacity to design and manage human experience. Theme parks leverage the principles of experience design to engage, inform, motivate, and inspire action, and create immersive, often transformational experiences.

Design for the entertainment industry is all about telling stories. However, unlike traditional theater, themed entertainment eliminates the fourth wall of the stage or screen, blurring the boundary between audience and performance, the audience itself becoming a player in the narrative — fully immersed in the direction, scope, and sequence (and associated emotion) of their journey. This bridges the gap between story and audience, creating spaces (physical, emotional, or virtual) where the performers/ storytellers and the audience share the experience together. Very much like healthcare.

When we design from this perspective, we are no longer tracking the patient's journey through spaces designed based on the organizing principles of the institution, but through the organizing principles of the patient's experience: the theme. Design then supports how we use space towards the transformative, thematic goal; thematic healthcare design can better support clinical operations and patient care.

*Healthcare Experience Design* is an approach to managing healthcare that examines the intention and purpose of systems of care and orchestrates interactions that optimize both process and outcomes for patients, families, and the professionals who share the work of worry about their health.

*Experience Design* is about understanding the factors that influence role-based interactions, decision-making, and relationships between people, products and services, and delivery channels. Experience design recognizes the power of tactile and emotive performance to effect engagement, acceptance, and commitment to healthcare goals — whether acute, chronic, or wellness-related — and accounts for their role in the day-to-day interactions and levels of affinity between patients, families, and their health-resource communities.

The principles and practices of experience design are ideally suited to create environments and systems of care that energize and support activation, engagement, and connection between patients, professionals, and the community in order to orchestrate and optimize transformative health-related experiences.

# 8

# Whole-Person/ Whole-Community Healthcare

ACHIEVING THE SOCIAL imperative of health will require a healthcare systems operating model that recognizes the whole-person, and the relationship between person and community, and acknowledges and supports our understanding of health as a multidimensional dynamic across all our levels of being: biomedical, environmental, social.

As described in detail by James Miller in his book, *Living Systems,* our well-being can be understood as harmony among our interrelated and interdependent levels of being. Taking a systems perspective on humanness, we exist not as independent biological entities, but as an entity composed of twelve hierarchical levels that are relentlessly interacting by sharing matter, energy, and information.

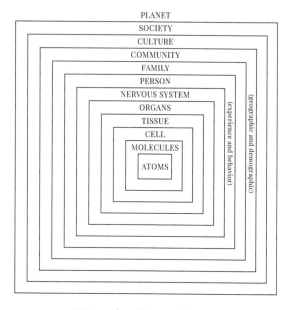

*Hierarchy of Living Systems*

Health or well-being is harmony within the hierarchy. Illness or disease is the result of a force or perturbation at one of the levels that reverberates among, and perturbs the function of, the whole. With this as the model for our understanding of health, the determinants of health become inclusive of, but not exclusive to, the etiologies of disease.

With this perspective on health as its foundation, the whole-person model for improving quality of health would incorporate a systems-level analysis of a person's condition, intervening where possible. In limiting our focus to molecular, cellular, and anatomic systems to the exclusion of a person's experience, behavior, community, and society, we sustain the historical reductionism of the medical model. Eliminating artificial boundaries related to the biopsychosocial determinants (molecular, physiological, structural, neuropsychological, environmental, genomic, biomic, or social) of a patient's conditions or risks would allow us to more accurately determine the functional requirements of systems to support achievement of the social imperative of health.

| SYSTEM LEVEL | CLINICAL STRATEGY | TACTIC |
| --- | --- | --- |
| Atoms | Radiation | Gamma Knife |
| Molecules | Biotechnology | Biologics |
| Cells | Genomics | Personalized Medicine |
| Tissues | Physiology | Pharmacology |
| Organs | Anatomic | Surgery |
| Nervous System | Plasticity | Biofeedback |
| Person (Experience and Behavior) | Wisdom | Reading |
| Family | Communication | Family Therapy |
| Community (Geographic and Demographic) | Advocacy | Medical–Legal Partnerships |
| Culture | Spiritual | Restorative Circles |
| Society | Government Affairs | Lobbying |
| Planet | Environmental Responsibility | Paris Agreement |

*Examples of Clinical Strategies across the Hierarchy of Systems*

## How Hierarchical Forces
## Shape Living Systems

In the modern era (18th-20th century) lead was introduced into our living system at the "society" level as an industrial product in paint and gasoline. Lead poisoning cases in children increased in cities (community level) in the 1950s and 1960s, having effects on their nervous and hematological systems. Their main source of exposure was particulate matter from emissions from cars and peeling lead-based paint in older housing stock. This disproportionately affected lower-income, minority families who were unable to take advantage of the suburban real-estate boom during that time. With the largely white flight to the suburbs determined by who could get mortgages, urban properties were purchased by landlords who neglected maintenance to increase their profit margins, resulting in peeling and flaking lead paint. At the same time, to support the increased use of cars to commute between city jobs and suburban homes, more highways were built through and around urban areas, leaving those disadvantaged families at even further risk. Combining granular lead paint chips and leaded dust from cars with the developmentally appropriate behavior of children to put things in their mouths equaled a public health crisis requiring research dollars, public policy changes, allocation of systemic resources, development of clinical resources, and new diagnostic and therapeutic modalities.

At the other end of the hierarchy, in Africa, a genetic mutation (molecular level) evolved in areas with endemic mosquito populations infected with Pasmodium, the parasite that causes malaria. This mutation caused a change in the shape of the person's red blood cells, protecting them from Pasmodium infection. Unfortunately, the new 'sickle' shape of red blood cells also has consequences, including severe pain, increased risk of infections, and anemia (impacting cells, tissues, and organs, as well as the nervous system). The key to understand risk for sickle cell anemia is at the family level, knowing whether parents are carriers and, as with lead poisoning, requiring investments and specific interventions at the clinical, community, and society levels.

Similar case studies can help us understand diverse health-related phenomenon such as the epidemic of type 2 diabetes, tobacco use, and the cause and consequence of food deserts.

## *Operationalizing Whole-Person Care*

Implementation of whole-person care requires a change in both the clinical operating model and the redesign of the implementation resource model to account for and effect goal-directed change towards the desired state at many levels of the hierarchy.

Care is not episodic, but lifespan-oriented. An individual's "plan of care" addresses the needs of the whole person. It is not static, but is continuously modified and optimized based on the dynamic nature of the human experience.

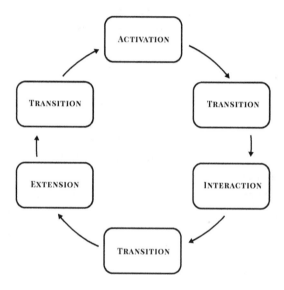

Care plan optimization begins with an activating event. Activation may be the result of a primary change at any level of the hierarchy, or a secondary change due to resultant ramifications of consequences at other levels. This could include the development of new symptoms;

the outreach of a member of their health resource community (based on the emergence of new data or a risk factor or to sustain healthcare maintenance); a scheduled event; or just a new aspirational desire originating from within the person.

Activation events are inevitably followed by some type of transition period; this may be the result of the event not yet recognized for its significance; lack of access to resources; health literacy; or the time required to clarify the event's significance or to search for the appropriate resources. People often pause and consider their options, priorities, and challenges before making a decision to act.

Once the activation event reaches a level of significance to the individual or community, some form of system-level interaction occurs; this could be a single, set, or series of interactions. These may or may not result in resolution; in complicated systems, there may be multiple dis-coordinated interactions. After system-level interaction, another transition period occurs; this may be 'discharge' from an encounter, a set of follow-up tasks associated with the interaction, or just a cooling off period.

However, just because the person has transitioned from the system does not mean the problem has transitioned from the person; their health status is inescapable. There is always a period of extension after interaction with systems of care, which under the best of circumstances means recovery, but there are no endings, just the transition period — which may be a quiet period, a processing period, or an incubating period — until the next activating event.

The primary focus of the social imperative is to create an individualized plan of care that addresses the patient's conditions at all levels of the hierarchy and is continually modified and optimized based on emerging activation events. Success will require a high level of affinity in order to move patient expectations away from the legacy of *sick care* and engage them around an aspirational plan of care that emphasizes prevention, risk reduction, and quality of health improvement, and accounts for, but is not dominated by, acute care needs.

The relationship begins with a *seven-step process that becomes the basis of a continual cycle of assessment and care plan modifications* based on changing and emerging needs.

### Step 1: Evaluate the individual's current condition: needs, strengths, current-state

The process begins with a person-first condition assessment, giving the individual the opportunity to voice their concerns, wishes, hopes, and dreams for their health. This is designed to build trust and ensure the patient's voice and personal story is heard and sustained throughout the development of their care plan. While there is an interview format, it is designed around open-ended questions and grounded in narrative. This needs assessment should be conducted by a trained interviewer, but not necessarily a licensed healthcare professional; whenever possible it is recorded and transcribed for text analysis.

The second component is a *person-level needs assessment.* This is a more formal strengths assessment designed to stratify the patient's capacity to accept, commit, and act upon a plan of care, including but not limited to: communication skills, motivation, coping skills, resilience, locus of control, and self-directedness. This can be completed independently or with coaching support. It also means taking into account how people sense, receive, and respond to information with subsequent, consequential challenges (and significance) to their functional and adaptive skills and patterns of behavior.

Finally, the patient's current-state and associated determinants of those conditions is assessed in categorical and non-categorical domains: physical and neuropsychological conditions, person-level behavior, functional capacity, burden index, and interactions related to family, community, and societal systems. This approach eliminates artificial boundaries related to the biopsychosocial determinants (molecular, physiological, structural, neuropsychological, behavioral, environmental, genomic, biomic, or social) of a patient's conditions or risks.

## Step 2: Determine the future-state goals

Under whole-person care, the patient's needs assessment and current state analysis are combined to create a proposed *Care Plan,* which defines immediate and long-term health-related person-level and system-level goals. The Care Plan also demonstrates how immediate-term recommendations relate to, build, or *ladder-up* to achieve the person-level goals as discovered in the person-level needs assessment, with special focus on reducing health and mental health risks and burden of illness, optimizing strengths, and enhancing functional capacity. The proposed Care Plan is presented to the patient for their review, approval, and acceptance; with acceptance and commitment to the Care Plan, it is shared across the patient's health-resource community. This Care Planning process can be completed independently by the patient on digital platforms, or with coaching by relationship managers or healthcare professionals.

## Step 3: Understand the determinants of the current condition

The dynamics of the patient's current condition are analyzed using the systems hierarchy, taking special care to define the relational frames of the physical, informational, and belief variables within and between the level of the hierarchy. This will allow for fully integrated multidimensional interventions.

## Step 4: Determine goal-directed strategies

A strategy is a conceptual framework that drives action — knowledge, attitudes, and behavior — in order to effect a change from *what is* to what should be. It is determined by the objectives that have been set and the circumstances and context in which that goal-directed action will take place.

With the patient's acceptance and commitment to the Care Plan, clinical strategies are explored using a shared decision-making model. While it is often not explicit under the current model of care, once a condition is targeted for intervention, a decision is made as to the clinical strategy that will ultimately determine the resources to be allocated for care. In medicine, we tend to think about this in terms of two choices: pharmacologic strategies via medications, or surgical strategies, which is the purposeful modification of someone's anatomy. The recent interest in behavioral and social/economic strategies gave rise to SDOH interventions.

Under whole-person health, the decision as to the clinical strategies is made an explicit step in the process, and the portfolio of strategies available to achieve Care Plan goals is much larger and often multi-channeled, with forces being applied simultaneously or orchestrated against different levels of the hierarchy at the same time. This is especially true as we are considering the influence of allostatic load on our capacity to improve quality of health.

Whole-person clinical strategies include, but are not limited to:

| Anatomical | Bioenergetic | Biomechanical | Biomic |
|------------|--------------|---------------|--------|
| Botanical | Environmental | Legal/Regulatory | Mind-body |
| Molecular | Movement | Nutrition | Spiritual |

## Step 5: Allocate resources to affect goal-directed change

Once the clinical strategies are determined, resource-allocation can take place: in one case it might be a prescription for a first-line antibiotic as the tactical realization of a pharmacologic strategy for strep throat; in another, the insertion of an intracranial pressure monitor as the action required under the surgical strategy for head trauma. Or, in yet another, it could be community action towards a source of pollution or legal action to abate a housing risk such as mold or lead paint. Resource allocation, however, takes a new direction under whole-person care.

Resource allocation under whole-person care is based on the concept of *dynamic resource allocation,* which refers to methods of continuously optimizing a configuration of assets

— matter, energy, and information — in order to maximize both effectiveness and efficiency of a goal-directed system. Dynamic resource allocation deals with changing inputs and environments which are highly dynamic and often difficult to estimate and predict, as future performance is not dependent on current state; very much like the health of human beings.

In this case, dynamic resource allocation is used as a process framework for managing the efficiency of resource-allocation toward optimal outcomes for patients. These resources may have different reward, benefit, and cost structures, where the most efficient are high-reward, high net-benefit, and low cost. Examples can range from the ability of Tai Chi to reduce the risk of falls, to the capacity to improve quality of life outcomes using emerging concepts of functional medicine, which promote health by addressing imbalances that can impair allostatic functions (assimilation, defense and repair, energy production, communication, and structural integrity) that result from gene-environment interactions, including lifestyle, environmental toxins, and the microbiome.

Based on the understanding of the patient's strengths, the initial resource recommendations are the highest efficiency, lowest cost resources as can be predicted by their attributes, beliefs, and functional status. Patients who are known to be highly motivated and self-directed can be directed towards self-service resources; other patients may require more human connection, and still others more institution-based resources.

Optimizing goal achievement is accomplished by monitoring the state of the patient's progress to goal, and escalating and de-escalating resources to effect productive changes in the patient's molecular, physiological, structural, neuropsychological, environmental, genomic, biomic, or social benchmarks.

## Step 6: Orchestrate the resource-community

We can increase the scope and power of care, and better ensure patient-centered success, by orchestrating the actions of a patient's health resource-community (irrespective of any formal affiliations or lack thereof) and managing the system-level context in which they work.

However, as we know from the symphony, orchestration is difficult without a common *score* that integrates the diverse instrumental voices while accounting for their different, but potentially harmonious, roles; equally, truly integrated care is impossible without a similar *single source of truth* for a patient's health-related goals and associated plans of care.

As such, whole-person care requires a universal framework for care planning, to serve as the single source of truth for a patient, aligning accountability across all the members of their health resource-community. A universal architecture for how we plan for care would integrate, and account for, acute, chronic, preventive, functional, and spiritual conditions, and would orient all the members of a patient's health resource-community toward the whole-person. It also allows for expansion of the health-resource community beyond the current boundaries of the healthcare system, incorporating family, friends, and community resources.

## Step 7: Monitor progress

Dynamic resource allocation dictates continuous monitoring of performance and progress towards a goal, with defined endpoints. Such endpoints may be fixed, as may occur in the management of an acute condition, or sustained, as in the case of a risk factor, or a chronic condition where the endpoint is some defined level of stability. Progress is benchmarked against thresholds that determine triggers to escalate, or de-escalate, resources.

*"Noise becomes data when it has a cognitive pattern. Data becomes information when assembled into a coherent whole, which can be related to other information. Information becomes knowledge when integrated with other information in a form useful for making decisions and determining actions. Knowledge becomes understanding when related to other knowledge in a manner useful in anticipating, judging and acting. Understanding becomes wisdom when informed by purpose, ethics, principles, memory and projection."*

–George Santayana, *The Life of Reason,* 1905

## Where expertise from outside of healthcare can enhance our capacity to turn data into knowledge

Except for devices like the EKG, healthcare does not have a standard set of scale and proportion by which to record the frequency of events. The use of non-standard scaled interval charts introduces both variance and interpretation bias in graphical representations of data and reduces consistency in decisions made with regard to understanding and acting on time-series data such as that collected for therapeutic progress.

Psychologist Ogden Lindsley created the Standard Celeration Chart (SCC) when he noted differences in the way teachers were charting behaviors under observation in the classroom. These differences interfered with therapeutic and pedagogical decision-making, as well as created inefficiencies, as the charts needs to be deciphered.

The SCC is a semi-logarithmic line chart that permits analysis of how changes occur over time. It can easily reflect relative and proportional change, depict and compare change in multiple quantities, as well as forecast and predict trends, all in a consistent, standardized interface and format. The SCC enables monitoring the derivative of the rate (i.e., the acceleration or deceleration), which means one is able to better adjust the nature of an intervention, and escalate or de-escalate resources, in order to optimize therapeutic progress.

## Sustaining Quality of Health

Whole-person care is a constantly cyclical process. Patient and community health status is constantly monitored, and clinical strategies and associated resources changed, escalated, or de-escalated depending on progress-to-goal. When specific goals are achieved, clinical strategies shift from improvement to maintenance. Care Plans are continually modified based on changes in the person's quality of health: their needs, aspirations, and dreams, as well as any changes in their acute, chronic, preventive, functional, and spiritual conditions.

## Whole-Person/Whole Community Economics

Achieving a social imperative for health will require a reconsideration of the economic models for public investments. First, the traditional funding siloes of health, education, and social services cannot be allocated in isolation, and investments in housing, employment, and infrastructure must support and prioritize the capacity of community fixtures and government to sustain the health and well-being of communities.

Second, we need to stop designing the way we deliver care around the way we pay for care; let's determine, as we have for education, what is an equitable level of care for everyone to get across their lifespan and ensure every American can access that level of care.

Third, we must recognize that, in the short term, we're going to have to invest heavily in undoing the otherwise preventable damage done to our nation by the way we've underserved American's health for the last thirty years.

# 9

# Behavioral Determinants of Health: Time for a New Basic Science?

HEALTHCARE ECONOMICS — financing, cost control, and payment reform — dominates our national conversation and has been the primary driver of care delivery redesign, especially around the emerging concept of *value-based care*. The growing prevalence of such models as the basis of measures of quality and outcomes has thrust the determinants of health beyond pharmacotherapies and surgery to the forefront of consideration. Variously called "social" or "non-medical" determinants, the influence of these factors is well-validated, although there has been some debate as to the extent to which the healthcare community should be held responsible for their role in a patient's quality of health.

However, among these determinants of health, there is no dispute as to the prominent effect of behavioral conditions and health-related behaviors on health status. Behavioral health has a history of being carved out from traditional medical care, but public health authorities attributed upwards of 40 percent of health status to individual behavior (vs. 10 percent of medical care). Healthcare providers and managed care systems are now working to acquire the capabilities to both manage behavioral health conditions, and effectively and efficiently assess and modify health-related behaviors among their patients and members.

To influence how social factors — housing, food insecurity — affect health resource utilization and common morbidities, health systems have created partnerships with community agencies to add social intervention services to the clinical armamentarium. Efforts to integrate behavioral health into mainstream clinical operations fall into two categories: managing neuropsychological conditions that have behavioral symptoms (such as depression and anxiety), and crafting interventions to address behavior as a determinant of health status in otherwise neurotypical patients (such as medication adherence, seat belt use, or healthier eating habits). Competencies in both areas are increasingly core to the successful practice of medicine across the lifespan.

However, outside of pharmacotherapy, mainstream medicine does not have a true, basic science foundation upon which to rest a rational and integrated approach to understanding and managing primary behavioral conditions, nor other health-related behaviors. Current approaches to managing health-related behaviors are focused on incorporating techniques such as motivational interviewing, positive psychology, and cognitive-behavior therapies, along with tools such as mobile apps, smart watches, and other monitors. While all these efforts have demonstrated directional progress, they do not provide a framework for an integrated model of care.

## One Opportunity for Knowledge Transfer: Behavior Analysis

However, there is a well-established and evidence-based framework for understanding and managing behavior that can support efforts towards care delivery redesign to achieve ambitious goals for both behavioral health and health-related behaviors: Applied Behavior Analysis (ABA).

Despite over 50 years of research, ABA is not a common therapeutic modality in the medical literature; as behavior analysts Keith Allen and Jeffrey Fine have noted:

*"Indeed, deciding where to publish studies addressing physical health conditions can pose a significant challenge for applied behavior analysts. To publish in the Journal of Applied Behavior Analysis (JABA), which values the methodological and conceptual systems of behavior analysis but is not widely read by the medical community, is to risk being ignored by the very audience most interested in the problems being studied."*

Applied Behavior Analysis (ABA) is a scientific discipline that uses the principles of behavior and learning theory to meaningfully effect positive and productive behavior change and demonstrate that the procedures used were directly attributable to the new behavior. ABA is not a single therapeutic approach, but a disciplined framework of highly individualized assessment and intervention strategies using continuous measurement, data-driven feedback, and procedure optimization. Behavior analysis relies on functional analysis and direct observation of treatment effects, and addresses both antecedents and reinforcers, as well as motivating operations or context of the behaviors being addressed.

ABA is sometimes criticized for a lack of large-scale clinical trials, but we need to be careful not to apply standards from pharmaceuticals to behavioral interventions, which are better evaluated based on single subject design, a model more aligned with the n-of-1 study model associated with personalized medicine. Single subject designs can be pressure-tested with reversals to and from baseline, multiple baselines, and successive addition or removal of components of treatment. The individual focus of single-subject trials permits true assessment of treatment effect and identification of characteristics that may alter treatment progress and outcomes. While there is a limited corpus of systematic large-scale replications of ABA studies, it is the body of evidence *in toto* that signifies the rigor and conduct of ABA in clinical practice across a wide range of conditions; this has been especially true for behavioral health.

One such body of widely accepted research relates to the success of ABA as evidence-based treatment for disabilities associated with Autism Spectrum Disorder (ASD). The resultant insurance reform in forty-six states mandating access to ABA for children with ASD has created a narrow perception of the indications for ABA. Nevertheless, the foundations of the discipline of behavior analysis, and its applications, are much broader, including, but not limited to, the documented capacity to address primary behavioral health conditions (ADHD, anxiety, depression, obsessive-compulsive disorder, feeding, and eating disorders), as well as severe behavior topographies such as self-injurious behavior, aggression, and both inborn and acquired brain disorders, such as Prader-Willi Syndrome, dementia, and traumatic brain injury. There are additional bodies of evidence demonstrating the potential of ABA to support positive, productive changes in health-related behaviors, including diet and nutrition, physical activity, sleep, substance abuse, safety, and medication adherence, as well as behavioral management of specific conditions such as asthma, high blood pressure, and diabetes. The principles of behavior analysis can also be used to define and pinpoint behavioral targets for therapeutic intervention, and more accurately measure the effectiveness and associated outcomes of pharmacotherapies, surgery, and rehabilitation services.

*Behavior analysis is just one of many "non-medical" disciplines that could serve as a foundation for the development of a rational approach to clinical strategies necessary to achieve the social imperative.*

When we refer to therapeutic modalities that target behavior as "non-medical," we only sustain the conceptual body-mind duality that has fragmented our capacity to deliver truly integrated care. The purview of medicine must be the whole person; limiting our modalities to molecular, cellular, and anatomic systems to the exclusion of a person's experience, behavior, community, and society puts unnecessary restrictions on our capacity to positively influence their quality of health.

Despite the arguments above, this essay is less about behavior analysis and more about the healthcare ecosystem supporting the introduction of what amounts to a new species, and overcoming resistance to disciplinary diversity.

Behavior analysis is just one of many "non-medical" disciplines that could serve as a foundation for the development of a rational approach to clinical strategies necessary to achieve the social imperative, analogous to the role germ theory has played in our efforts to combat infectious disease. Partnering with behavior analysts in the same way we partner with microbiologists, biochemists, and physiologists could be a critical success factor in our capacity to achieve the true value of behavioral integration in the evolution of healthcare's clinical operating model.

# 10

# Brown M&Ms

MEDICAL SCHOOL MAY have sidetracked my career as an entertainer, but theater and music have remained very important to me personally. I also happen to have many friends who ended up in the music business, and I have always loved hanging around with them (and have fond memories of a particular 1997 Grammy Awards afterparty).

One of the funniest aspects of the music business is the *artist rider* — which is a set of requests or demands that musical artists set as criteria for performing. It is often technical (must have a Steinway piano or a certain type of microphone), or personnel related, but can also be related to hospitality requests, such as certain types of food or beverages, towels, and other stuff.

One of the most famous rider clauses was the "brown M&M" clause in the Van Halen contract. It stipulated that a bowl of M&Ms was to be present in the dressing room, with all the brown M&Ms removed. Failure to place the bowl, or to remove the brown ones, would result in the band not performing and full payment required.

Band member David Lee Roth wrote in his autobiography that the band really didn't care about the brown M&Ms—they used the clause as an indicator of the level of attention to detail at a concert venue. They did not trust others to pay as much attention to detail as the band did, so they set some tasks as indicators. Brown M&Ms? Chances are the microphones were in the wrong place too. No brown M&Ms? The drums were probably set up properly.

This rings true to me because other well-known musicians, actors, and athletes I have known have endorsed the theory. These people perform in an elite emotional space—their concentration, focus, and capacity for performing is completely dependent on finding a secure mental space from which to do their work. They tend to worry about not being in the right mental space when they need to perform, so they set about creating criteria — in the form of requests or demands — of those around them to assure and check that they are secure and protected from distractions and surprises.

I was reminded of this when I was the chief medical officer for a national primary care network, because some of our clinicians were having trouble trusting that our system of care had the right attention to detail, and their worries left them feeling isolated and insecure. I wish there were a bowl of M&Ms I could point to and say, "Hey, we got this."

The problem is that these clinicians do not represent an isolated case. Healthcare professionals are a lot like these elite performers and have a lot of trouble trusting others to have the same level of attention to detail as they do. They work in a very unique mental space, require a secure base to work from, and are easily pulled off their game by distractions (especially if the distractions conflict with their sense of professional identity).

> I wish there were a bowl of M&Ms I could point to and say, "Hey, we got this."

Health professionals are, by and large, big worriers; we are an anxious bunch. However, our worries are professional in nature, rather than personal. Due to our training and temperament, we are more inclined to worry about others than ourselves. In fact, I would submit that the foundation of successful healthcare is not the scientific method, but a willingness to truly shoulder the work of worrying about another, unrelated, human being.

Trained to root out often well-hidden pathology, and fearful of making life-changing (or life-taking) mistakes, we rarely accept that what we see is all that there is to know; our raison d'etre as a profession is to root out these things and, when we can, fix them. Doctors, nurses, and pharmacists invest lifetimes to try and understand "humanness" — often deconstructing and disassembling people into their smallest (sometimes atomic) parts to learn how those parts are supposed to, but sometimes don't, work or interact. This knowledge helps us find the best-fit structural or physiological solutions for challenges to health and/or managing illness.

To a physician, even when we think we know what's going on, there's the fear that something else may be lurking. Although we never admit it, even when we finally make a decision, we are unconsciously terrified all the time; there is always a looming threat that some obscure or otherwise unpredicted variation in humanness will turn our carefully thought-through and experience-matched clinical strategies into biological disasters.

## Stable Clinicians, Stable Health

Medical training — both medical school and residency — is designed to wire our brains this way. That's largely because, even in an era when almost 70 percent of physicians are salaried employees, the context of training remains trapped in its historical endgame: solo practice, hanging out a shingle without any supervision or oversight, and taking responsibility for the well-being of a few thousand people. Hence our terror: we're programmed to be loners.

That's why we're inside our heads so much of the time, riddled with self-doubt but putting on a game face for the social environment. Our brains are a calculus of probabilities, facts, and qualitative assessments, and are constantly absorbing new information to factor into our thought-flow. It's a relentless and exhausting quest, saddled with the burden of lifelong learning, relearning, and unlearning. Imagine waking up every day of your career and discovering something you learned is now wrong!

I don't know anyone that went to medical school to get rich. For those with the academic rigor necessary for medical school admission, there are many other options for generating wealth that do not involve urine, stool, and vomitus. This is not to say that economics is not part of the equation; but for most medical students, aspiring to be a physician is largely driven by intrinsic motivations: the challenge of intellectual and technical mastery, the capacity to positively change people's lives, professional autonomy, and the social capital associated with the place of the physician in community and society.

From an economic perspective, a medical career is far more about financial security than accumulation of capital. Those that grew up in modest circumstances may be *richer* than where they came from, but are not wealthy (especially if you train in pediatrics); for those that came from families of real means, even the upper echelons of medical practice would barely give them parity with their social strata.

One of the fundamental requirements of a successful career as a healthcare professional is the sense that your efforts — your studies, your discipline, your mastery, and your work of worry — will be channeled to achieve some form of positive results for your patient, and be valued by the community. By treating healthcare professionals as production workers, rather than elite athletes, we undermined their intrinsic motivations, removed the economic stability that supported selfless behavior, snubbed their normative needs for recognition and respect, and fragmented their sense of professional community. This has not served patients, nor the professionals themselves, very well.

In their 2014 book, *Scarcity*, Harvard economist Sendhil Mullainathan and Princeton cognitive psychologist Eldar Shafir make a compelling case for how the perception of threat to personal resources has a significantly adverse effect on cognitive function. While neither of their work focused on the correlation between poverty and counterproductive behaviors, subsequent work demonstrated that the concept of threat was relative and independent of income or even wealth; adverse neuropsychological consequences can be triggered simply by the perception of looming or impending peril.

As Mullainathan and Shafir make clear, it is very hard to sustain your desire and commitment to care about others when you perceive your own well-being as threatened. It may seem dissonant to consider the well-being of professionals who live well above the poverty line, but, while the motivation and context for their commitment may transcend economics, financial stability is critical to healthcare professionals because it provides the secure base from which they can pursue non-economic goals such as the lifelong learning, demands of professional life, and have the emotional capacity to shoulder the work of worry about the well-being of others. In other words, people who are forced to worry about their own well-being are generally not able to invest as much in the lives of others.

*It is very hard to sustain your desire and commitment to care about others when you perceive your own well-being as threatened.*

All health professionals take on an extraordinary depth of responsibility for other people's lives. As such, their confidence, optimism, and professionalism must be nurtured and protected; these elements — critical to successful performance of their duties — cannot survive when left exposed to the elements. Our society seems to understand this dynamic when it comes to the performance of our elite athletes and entertainers, but we can't seem to make the same respectful accommodations to the critical performance of those we entrust with our health and our lives.

A study in the proceedings of the National Academy of Sciences examined the careers of West Point graduates and noted that for those with intrinsic motivations, adding an extrinsic motivator like money was more of a negative influence on their career success and satisfaction. This can explain why doctors — even when employed — don't respond to the same kinds of economic stimuli as business people.

Clinicians are professionals first. We expect them to operate at levels of elite performance, but we don't always design our management style around their needs as elite performers. This is not about special treatment or allowing bad behavior, but about making sure our systems of practice are appropriately responsive to the cultural mindset and commitments that they bring to their role, and that we leverage to our advantage as a business every day.

And I have found that by doing so — by making sure they understand that they are safe, secure, valued, and respected — they will trust us more, be more open and more fully engaged in the organization, and be more available to share the work of worry with their patients.

## 11

# Moonshot: "I do not think it means what you think it means"

WHEN I WAS chief medical officer of a national primary care network and ACO, I was regularly contacted by entrepreneurs who had no doubt that their product, service, invention, or Big Idea was exactly what my organization needed to increase revenue, improve quality, engage patients, add value, or reduce costs. From my own entrepreneurial experience, I recognize and empathize with their vision and passion.

However, there were flaws in their logic. First, they had a presumption of our ignorance: having made their magical discovery, they would inadvertently discount the depth of our experience and insights. Second, the fallacy of profundity: the assumption that solving a relatively narrow problem would have a transformational effect on our organization, or the system at large.

These feelings came back to me recently when I saw a new "Moonshot Investing" program that was to be announced at the annual JP Morgan Healthcare Conference in San Francisco.

For those who may not know, there is a parallel world of healthcare, separate from those who provide patient care, composed of angel investors, private equity firms, and venture capitalists. Inventors and entrepreneurs configure their prototypes and plans and, like ligands seeking a receptor, approach their boundary. If they connect, the entrepreneurs are translocated into the startup universe (or scale-up universe, for established companies seeking growth), where their business DNA is activated and their operational phenotype is matured, until they are ready to be actively transported into the marketplace. Most entrepreneurs require multiple attempts before they find the right receptor; many never make a match.

For 30-plus years, the invitation-only JP Morgan Healthcare Conference (JPM) has been a major node in this universe. Along the way, another ecosystem sprung up alongside—thousands come to San Francisco at the same time as JPM not to attend, but to make deals. This is where the Moonshot Investing announcement took place.

I have great respect for start-up culture and know many for whom the supportive nature of the start-up community has been absolutely crucial in getting their company off the ground. However, using the theme of "Moonshots" has revealed what might be a fatal flaw — and a dangerous risk — associated with startup culture.

The Moonshot analogy is used when people want to allude to the overwhelming ambition and sheer audacity of a goal. Harkening back to the space race, moonshots are previously-considered impossible missions, undertaken with some risk of failure, in order to deliver unprecedented results.

Among the 80-plus companies designed as "moonshots," there were some with great potential to contribute to quality of care and quality of health. The problem is that there is no audacity among them. There is nothing that could genuinely be called a "moonshot," even if taken collectively. Do we really need another health coach? Is that app really transformational?

*Most of these companies developed elegant solutions to problems that are actually grounded in design flaws in our current system.*

Most of these companies developed elegant solutions to problems that are actually grounded in design flaws in our current system. Others reflect medicine's reductionist nature, with the hope that attacking the pieces might heal the whole. And while entrepreneurs should be lauded for their spirit, aligning startup culture with moonshot-level transformation ends up making them look like they are wearing the emperor's new clothes.

There's an apocryphal story about President John Kennedy visiting NASA and asking a janitor what he was doing; he responded, "I'm helping put a man on the moon." True or not, this story reflects the underlying spirit of a moonshot: alignment among diverse stakeholders towards a singular vision.

Moonshots are transcendent. A moonshot makes you want to sacrifice your career to be part of something bigger than yourself. A moonshot is about creating something that, as artist Walter Sickert has said, "Makes it impossible for those who follow to ever act as if it has not existed."

With this, the start-up movement may have gone too far, encouraging passionate, innovative people to leave the healthcare talent pool to focus on their own ideas, even when they might make a bigger contribution by bringing their insights to something bigger or bolder.

A moonshot requires coordinated innovation in service of the Big Goal. A more accurate application of the moonshot mentality would have investors using their money to convince many of the smart, passionate, and energetic entrepreneurs to reconsider their own ventures and contribute to one that could achieve a level of change otherwise impossible without them.

New ideas are not necessary for a moonshot; people imagined space travel for eons before we finally lifted off. A moonshot should not necessarily have an immediate rate of return, and it should contribute far beyond its immediate achievement.

In 1977, Dr. George Engel raised the specter of reductionism in medicine and advocated for a more inclusive scientific model. Dr. Engel wrote, "Physicians in the future are to apply the same scientific rigor to the approach and understanding of patients and their care as they customarily apply to the diagnosis and treatment of disease." His recommendations were prescient, yet we have done little substantive work towards their realization. Much of what we consider innovation today would be superfluous if we had taken Dr. Engel's advice to incorporate behavioral dimensions and social factors into our model for care.

*Much of what we consider innovation today would be superfluous if we had taken Dr. Engel's advice to incorporate behavioral dimensions and social factors into our model for care.*

Let's not fall into the reductionist trap that diminishes the concept and impact of a moonshot. It can't just be about creating a critical mass of good ideas against a problem. It should be something that seems almost, well... *inconceivable!*

# 12

# What Can Healthcare Learn from Art History?

**DAVID GALENSON IS** a world-class economic researcher and professor at the University of Chicago, who also happens to have deep interest in the process of innovation. In his book, *Conceptual Revolutions in Twentieth Century Art,* Dr. Galenson applied some of his substantial research skills to art history and the phenomenon of creative change. What's interesting is there are whole parts of the book in which we could just cross out "art" or "artist" and "20th century," and replace them with the words "medicine," "physician," and "21st century," and the points would be equally valid and powerful. This is especially true when examining the acceptance of innovation, the role and influence of peers in managing creative change, and what Galenson calls the "rate of change."

Ahead are a few *"excerpts from the book,"* along with some parallel thoughts with regard to the world of healthcare:

> *"Innovation has always been the distinguishing feature of important art, but the need for innovation to be conspicuous is a particular hallmark of the modern era, and the pace of change has accelerated within that era."*

We all know the quoted studies on how it takes twenty-plus years for valid research findings to become accepted as standards of care. But in today's healthcare, the phenomenon of innovation extends beyond considerations of diagnosis and treatment to the very nature of the profession, roles, responsibilities, relationships, models of collaboration, and tool sets. And the demands on individuals and systems to change have become immense. This was also the case in the transition in art in the early 20th century; for decades, stylistic change was glacial, and periods or "movements" were well established. Before 20th-century art, a painter of Picasso's power and influence would never have changed style; yet change was Picasso's raison d'etre. Today in healthcare, we see lots of forced change under the guise of innovation. It will be interesting to see which of those changes will constitute "true" innovations with lasting effect. Of course, the art world didn't have multi-billion-dollar federal programs and a private equity community pushing certain forms of innovation over others. As to whether innovation can be forced, Galenson's opinion can be summed up in this quote:

> *"In 1965, Harold Rosenberg, who was himself a leading critic, conceded that 'Manipulated fame exists, of course, in the art world.' Yet he emphasized that this fame was fleeting: 'The sum of it is that no dealer, curator, buyer, critic or any existing combination of these, can be depended upon to produce a reputation that is more than a momentary flurry.' Real power in the art world came from only one source: 'the single most potent force in the art world is still, in the last analysis, the artist.'"*

The open question is whether venture backed innovation is really just "momentary flurry." A bigger question, however, is what will remain or what will evolve if, to paraphrase Rosenberg, "the single most potent force in healthcare is still, in the last analysis, the clinician"?

Galenson noted:

> *"Important artists are innovators whose work changes the practices of their successors. The greater the changes, the greater the artist. It is those artists who have the greatest influence on their peers – and the artists of later generations – whose work hangs in major museums, becomes the subject of study by scholars, and sells for the highest prices."*

Galenson quotes painter Walter Sickert:

> *"Perhaps the importance that we must attach to the achievement of an artist or a group of artists may properly be measured by the answer to the following question: Have they so wrought that it will be impossible henceforth, for those who follow, ever again to act as if they had not existed?"*

True in medicine up to a point: names like Semmelweis, Lister, Pasteur, Osler, Salk, Penfield, and Freud all fit the criteria. But we have lost, or fragmented, the idea of influencers at these levels. These days true innovation, if it happens at all, happens within specialties or with an eye towards an exit, not across the overall professional identity of physicians as a class. Who among our peers today is doing work that will forever change the way we think about medicine? Have we restricted our growth as a profession by limiting the innovation paths between and across disciplinary boundaries? And how do we treat our innovators?

*Who among our peers today is doing work that will forever change the way we think about medicine?*

> *"Significant artistic innovators are of course not simply initially unappreciated: they are vigorously*

*attacked. Any innovative new art form necessarily involves the rejection of older values. For practitioners and admirers of those older values, this causes "a sense of loss, of sudden exile, of something willfully denied . . . a feeling that one's accumulated culture or experience is hopelessly devalued." It is hardly surprising that those committed to established forms refuse to accept innovations that would make those forms obsolete, and thus cause a devaluation of their own knowledge and skills. This phenomenon is not unique to art, but in scholarship is known as Planck's principle, named for the physicist Max Planck, who observed that "a new scientific truth does not triumph by convincing its opponents and making them see the light, but rather because its opponents eventually die, and a new generation grows up that is familiar with it."*

I hope Planck's sentiment is not true, but I have unfortunately experienced the vociferous Kubler-Rossian anger of some physicians because of something as simple as an unexpected demand on their intellectual attention. The very existence of threats to retire due to changes in the form and function of the practice of medicine reflects an entrenched reactionary position and is a sad commentary on the lack of capacity of an entire generation of physicians to organically evolve their professional identity.

"*Examples of great artists who evolved from youthful revolutionaries into aging reactionaries are not difficult to find. Leo Castelli opened an art gallery in New York in 1957, and only a year later presented Jasper Johns' first one-man exhibition, which was an immediate sensation in the art world. Castelli became the leading art dealer of the 1960s and 1970s, representing Johns, Robert Rauschenberg, the major Pop artists — notably Andy Warhol, Roy Lichtenstein, and Claes Oldenburg — as well as such younger stars as Frank Stella, Richard Serra, and Bruce Nauman. In an interview in 1994, Castelli recalled his dismay when the 1993 Whitney Biennial exhibition had forced him to recognize the impact of new developments that had been occurring in advanced art, with the increased use of new media, including video, and the prominence of younger German and Italian painters: 'I had to accept the fact that the wonderful days of the era I had participated in, and in which I had played a substantial role, were over.' He initially could not accept the legitimacy of the newer art: 'I felt that what had been there before, during the great era of the sixties, was unbeatable, and that nothing of that kind could succeed the heroic times that we had had here in New York.' On reflection, however, he realized that he had to accept the new art, so that he would not repeat the universal error of aging art experts: 'There was a certain sadness that I felt about it, but well, with the Whitney show, I realized that I had to change my attitude, and not be rejecting — as people generally are, as you know. I would say that there is a span, a relatively short span, in which somebody really lives seriously with a period of art and after that, all those people — whether it be dealers or art historians or museum directors — after that they don't see what's going on anymore. They reject whatever comes after that. I didn't want to be one of those.'"*

Despite nearly forty years having passed since my medical school graduation, in my mind I am still an 'early career' physician, but I did find myself recently telling a "When I was your age" story to some genuinely early career physicians about what life was like being on call for 36-plus hours straight every third night. And despite whatever objective criteria were the basis of such changes in residency training, at a very basic level, I believe there was something significant lost in the transition. Comparing my experience to theirs, I completely understand what Castelli was saying when he felt that "What had been there…was unbeatable, and nothing of the kind could succeed the heroic times we had." Per Galenson:

*"Significant innovations inevitably impose losses on those who cherish the values the new innovations reject, but of course they also offer gains. The artistic innovators who are faced with attacks on their new*

methods understand this. For example, Kazimir Malevich remarked in 1919 that "People always demand that art be comprehensible, but they never demand of themselves that they adapt themselves to comprehension." When artists create significant new forms of art, they almost invariably see their innovations denounced by critics who are judging their new methods by the rules or conventions of earlier art, which the innovators have intentionally discarded. Thus in 1914, Wassily Kandinsky warned against critics who claimed to have found flaws in new art: "one should never trust a theoretician (art historian, critic, etc.) who asserts that he has discovered some objective mistake in a work." Kandinsky explained that, in ignorance of the purpose of the new work, the detractor was invariably applying outmoded criteria: "The only thing a theoretician is justified in asserting is that he does not yet know this or that method. If in praising or condemning a work theoreticians start from an analysis of already existing forms, they are most dangerously misleading." Ideally a critic would take care to understand the new methods of the innovative new work, then explain it to a wider

"People always demand that art be comprehensible, but they never demand of themselves that they adapt themselves to comprehension."

*audience: "he would try to feel how this or that form*
*works internally, and then he would convey his total*
*experience vividly to the public."*

And this is even worse with physicians, who are cognitively trained and culturally oriented to finding pathology. You cannot get in front of a group of doctors with a new idea — even one with gobs of rational scientific data behind it — and expect it to be accepted. They are compelled to poke, prod, dissect, and otherwise deconstruct it to find the flaws. And they approach every problem with the presumption that whatever is seen on the surface is hiding some weakness or imperfection; because the worst thing a physician can do is miss something that is wrong. There is an additional problem when they are asked to evaluate or assess the value of something that is based on principles with which they are unfamiliar; rather than say "Gee, help me understand how this works," they make analogies to the familiar, and allow those outmoded criteria to run their judgment. Galenson again:

*"Yet the difficulty of understanding innovative*
*new art has increased over the course of the modern*
*era, because of the increasing prominence of highly*
*conceptual art. Understanding advanced art would*
*subsequently be primarily intellectual rather than*
*visual: "An advanced painting of this century inevitably*
*gives rise in the spectator to a conflict between his eye*

> *and his mind; as Thomas Hess has pointed out, the*
> *fable of the emperor's new clothes is echoed at the birth*
> *of every modernist art movement. If work in a new*
> *mode is to be accepted, the eye/mind conflict must be*
> *resolved in favor of the mind; that is, of the language*
> *absorbed into the work."*

I'll let Picasso take this one: "The fact that for a long-time cubism has not been understood and that even today there are people who cannot see anything in it, means nothing. I do not read English; an English book is a blank book to me. (But) this does not mean that the English language does not exist. Why should I blame anybody else but myself if I cannot understand what I know nothing about?"

The future of medicine lies in our ability and willingness to absorb and be changed by new ideas. As Galenson wrote:

> *"In part, the difficulty at issue here is simply that*
> *of assimilating innovative new art in a period of*
> *rapid change."*

Or, "In part, the difficulty at issue here is simply that of assimilating innovative [new approaches to the art of medicine] in a period of rapid change."

# 13

# Systems Design for the Social Imperative

ONE OF THE foundational principles of medicine is rational therapeutics, in which our understanding of the structure, function, and mechanics of human biology and behavior is leveraged in the design of interventions to attenuate or ameliorate biomedical or structural pathology and reduce health-related risks. We have not applied the same discipline to the design of our systems of care.

With this as a backdrop, let's be clear that systems (such as our current healthcare ecosystem) that evolve organically cannot have a clear reason for being and, as such, often contain minefields of conflicting priorities, resulting in nodes of achievement but no overarching integrity of purpose.

Achieving the social imperative of health will require a transformational approach to healthcare delivery that shifts the focus from *caring* for patients who have active conditions or self-select for care to *taking* on transcendent responsibility for the health of our communities.

Under the social imperative, success is more than a full waiting room and busy switchboard. When system-level achievement is based on the capacity to effect measurable change at the community-level, patients who do not identify as needing care may require a different level of consideration than those who request it.

*Under the social imperative, success is more than a full waiting room and busy switchboard.*

A system is more than a collection of objects. True systems are organized around some kind of binding processes. In order to function as a system, even higher-order collections (clustering of collections) require some organizing principles that bind its elements and provide a framework for relations and patterns, supporting the system's goal-directed intent.

Similarly, an understanding of the *basic science* of systems design will be essential for the development of a rational system to achieve the social imperative for health.

## The Basic Science of Systems Design

The basic science of healthcare systems design is grounded in two disciplines: functional analysis and socio-technical systems design.

Functional analysis, as represented by the Functional Resonance Analysis Method (FRAM) used by the aerospace industry to understand risk in dynamic systems, is used to identify the functional areas that are critical to achieve the goals or tasks of the system. Healthcare has typically focused on system structures (such as discipline-based departments) rather than system functions. Functional analysis produces a model that defines what is needed for everyday performance to go right. The key is to identify the functional *requirements* of the system: those elements which, if not fulfilled or realized, will limit the potential for goal achievement.

While all functional requirements must be fulfilled, individual organizations may apply different technical, organizational, social, and human factors to fulfill them and achieve system-level goal achievement. Socio-technical systems

*The key is to identify the functional requirements of the system: those elements which, if not fulfilled or realized, will limit the potential for goal achievement.*

engineering (STSE) is a methodology that supports the specifications, design, operation, evaluation, and evolution of complex systems. Based on its capacity to support the functional requirements, STSE starts with the intent and purpose of an experience, and orchestrates interactions, roles, sequences of events, decisions, and configurations between various programs, platforms, partners, and personnel.

STSE integrates human, social, and organizational factors, as well as technical factors, into the design of our systems of care. It is a people-first methodology to make interactions with complex systems more efficient, effective, pleasant, or meaningful.

The use of STSE has been perfected in industries that are able to use a combination of sophisticated technologies and human services to build deep connections and trust with their audiences, despite complex large-scale operations that must deliver value while safely serving thousands of diverse audiences daily, such as theme parks, museums, and cultural attractions. Like healthcare, these industries depend heavily on quality, operational performance, infrastructure, and logistics for their success, but they also put equal discipline into managing the human experience in order to engage, inform, motivate, and inspire action, and create immersive, often transformative, experiences.

Let's explore a system design framework drawn from these two methodologies.

The operating model of any successful system is comprised of three highly interrelated components:

1. A set of *functional requirements* supporting the overarching goal(s) of the intended system and how they will be fulfilled.

2. An understanding and mastery of the *operating capabilities* that allow those functions to be fully realized.

3. An *interaction design* that orchestrates the operating capabilities and their interface with other environmental factors and forces.

## Example: Designing a Vehicle

What are the *functional requirements* of a vehicle?

First, you need a source of power and a method of transmission of the power to move the vehicle. You need a capacity to accelerate and decelerate, and you need some system for directional management. As we will see, the functional requirements can be fulfilled and accounted for in different ways; how those requirements are fulfilled will determine the size, shape, and type of vehicle: car, boat, motorcycle, or even bicycle. However, the system, represented in this case by a vehicle of some type, cannot operate successfully in the world without all of its functional requirements being accounted for and met in one way or another.

For all vehicle types, the *operating capabilities* for driving require mastering vehicle-specific methods of acceleration, deceleration, and directional management. However, the operating capabilities (as well as the competency of the driver) are dependent on how the functional requirements are met and fulfilled. In the case of an automobile or motorcycle, the source of power may be an internal combustion or electric engine. However, the operational similarities end there: for a car, the method of acceleration and braking are pedals operated by the right foot; transmission may be automatic or manual (requiring additional mastery of left foot to operate the clutch and right hand to navigate the gearshift). Directional control is via a steering wheel. In contrast, on a motorcycle, there is a right-handed twist grip for acceleration and combination of right hand (front wheel) and right foot (rear wheel) brakes; there is a manual left-hand clutch and a transmission operated by the left foot. Motorcycle steering is via handlebars which control a front forked wheel, whereas bicycles are human powered, can have hand brakes or foot brakes, and may be single or multiple-geared. In addition to the operating capabilities associated with each of the functional requirements, there are additional competencies required in terms of rules of the road — symbol recognition — and vehicle maintenance. And, in the case of the bicycle, balance and fitness.

Operating capabilities are generally not intuitive and should always be practiced, mastered, tested, and benchmarked before attempting any form of production-level performance. Acquiring the capacity to drive a vehicle is a tangible skill requiring physical practice; deep understanding of how the brakes work does not confer the skills required to operate them. Nor can the skills be automatically transferred between vehicles that have different expressions of the functional requirements.

This is equally true for the operating model of playing a musical instrument: while the functional requirements include knowing how to read music, an understanding of rhythm and some methodology of sound production, the operating capabilities of fingering (and, on occasion, breath control) for each note is different, and not easily transferable, between instruments. You can understand the physics of the saxophone but still not be able to play a note.

This is the fundamental issue as we set out to achieve the social imperative; we can talk about it theoretically but it's in the rehearsal, the practice, and the mastery of these operating capabilities that the achievement takes place.

So what does it take to drive the vehicle? Even after mastering the operating capabilities, there is a *designed orchestration of interactions* between discrete capabilities and, overall, with the environment: you have to master the operating capabilities, follow the rules of the road, and interact with other vehicles. This has its foundation in a capacity to collaborate and integrate operating capabilities with knowledge of the rules of the road and spatial-perceptual skills.

So there are three components to the *interaction design:*

1. **Your own interaction with the vehicle.**

2. **The interaction between you and the operating rules of the road.**

3. **The real-time improvisational interaction with the other vehicles.**

While driving or playing an instrument is an individual activity, operating models for systems and their components are also applicable at the organizational level. In other words, the capacity of the organization — through its people and processes — to meet functional requirements is an independent variable that must be addressed. This cannot be assumed to be an inherent or native capability among the existing role and team-related operating capabilities; existing or prior roles in the organization may not align under the new goal-directed functional requirements.

## Systems Design for the Social Imperative

A system of care in which the purpose and intent is to *improve quality of health in order to enhance the capacity of individuals to contribute — emotionally, socially, and economically — as active, productive members of family and community* has a unique set of functional requirements, associated operating capabilities, and interaction design. These are different from, but inclusive of, those from traditional medical practice and are based on achieving measurable outcomes that will require competencies that are not native to healthcare as it is known today.

There are a couple of very fundamental competencies that are required when you start to take transcendent responsibility for a cohort, one of which is you have to reach out and find people who need care, even though they themselves have not acknowledged that they need care. You need to bring them into the care system, engage them in a care planning process, and engage them in the behavior and attitude change that's required to achieve some mutually agreed upon goals. Here are those three components in further detail.

## Phase 1: Define and Fulfill the Functional Requirements

Figure 1 (see next page) outlines the nine universal functional requirements for systems-based practice for the social imperative.

How these requirements are accounted for and fulfilled is the first critical success factor in the design of systems intended to achieve the social imperative of health. If you have not fulfilled all of the functional requirements in one way or another, your system will fail. It could fail small, it could fail big, but it will fail.

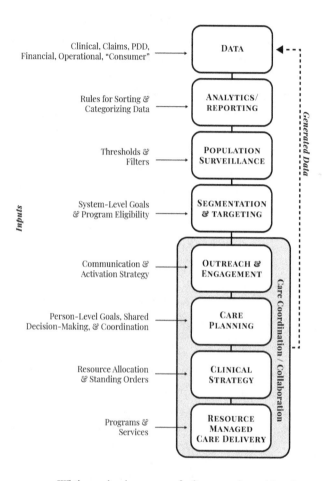

While technology can facilitate and enable these functional requirements, the social imperative is not necessarily technology-dependent. In fact, according to the principles of socio-technical systems engineering, systems are often designed to meet technical requirements but fail because they do not account for the human factors — tactile, emotive, cognitive, and conative — that affect their capacity to fully realize the person-level or organizational goals.

It is the combination of functional strategy and the operational workflow between these elements — how they work together, technologically enabled or not — that creates the structural integrity of a system. While many organizations have existing resources and assets that can be repurposed and optimized to meet these functional requirements, there are some requirements — such as engagement, activation, and collaboration — that may require some new programmatic or organizational competencies.

Let's examine each functional requirement:

## Data

The type of data you need depends on the outcomes you are seeking to achieve and is determined by the metrics of success or benchmarks of outcomes and the degree to which you will understand the experiences of the individuals and communities you serve. Predetermining the data (based on what's already available or easily accessible, for example) will introduce bias into your system's performance. Data choices must reflect the current state of the individuals you serve, their families, and communities, as well as the operational performance of your node in the system and the system as a whole. Data can be quantitative or qualitative; structured or unstructured. In healthcare, lived experience should be considered data. The social imperative will require types of data that may not be traditionally considered "healthcare" data, such as consumer behavior patterns, or perhaps even new types of data altogether.

## Analytics/Reporting

Analytics is the process by which insights are derived from data. Fundamentally, analytics is about understanding the interrelationship between metrics in order to guide goal-directed decisions or actions; analytics can provide historical, current, and predictive views of those being served, as well as the operations and performance of the system or subsystem under observation. The types and methods of analysis or modeling are grounded in the purpose and intent of the system and should 'ladder up' to strategically support the envisioned future state of the community.

## Surveillance

Taking transcendent responsibility for the health of a community requires the capacity to identify needs and recognize individuals and families in need. Expanding the scope of the traditional model of public health surveillance to support the social imperative will allow for targeting of individuals as well as proactive, upstream interventions at the community level.

Filters and thresholds are defined that allow for recognition of trends in the community that indicate, or predict, risk or changes in condition.

## Segmentation and Targeting

Members of the community are segmented based on their current state of health, but also their known attributes and channel preferences, life stage, etc. Based on this segmentation, they are targeted for individualized care planning, and supportive or transformational interventions. Patients can also be stratified by activation level or 'impactibility.'

## Outreach and Engagement

Optimized communication strategies will close the loop on care planning and paths towards goal achievement. Communication is not currently a fundamental skill or competency of healthcare. This is not to say that there aren't individuals or organizations who communicate well, but it's not a discipline of the profession, and that spills over to our systems of care. Engagement, similarly, is not necessarily a competency. Industry has mastered the tools, techniques, and strategies to engage; healthcare needs to master certain core competencies in order to manage cohorts rather than individuals in one-on-one care.

## Care Planning

Once the patients are engaged, additional 'person-level' goals are added to the care plan via a shared decision-making framework, and patient-centered clinical strategies are determined. Care planning focuses on goals: what we will change or reinforce.

This care plan becomes the "single source of truth" across all members of the individual's health resource-community.

## Clinical Strategy

Based on the *whole-person model of care,* intervention planning is broken up into two distinct phases: strategy and delivery, all based on identified determinants of the patient's current state and the identified future state. Strategies are the conceptual frameworks that serve as drivers of goal-directed change. They serve as the basis of actionable decisions. For example, for a biomedical condition, are we choosing a pharmacologic or surgical strategy? Once the strategy is determined, decisions can be made as to the specific tactical or programmatic resources that will be deployed to realize the strategy.

## *Care Delivery*

Care delivery involves orchestrating goal-directed allocations of resources to effect change in health status or to support a plan of care to sustain or improve the quality of health of individuals. It should be treated as a process framework for managing the efficiency of resource-allocation toward optimal outcomes for individuals and communities. This is accomplished by monitoring the state of the patient's risks and conditions, and escalating and de-escalating clinical and other resources to effect productive changes in the patient's health status and molecular, physiological, structural, neuropsychological, environmental, genomic, biomic, or social benchmarks.

## *Collaboration*

Collaboration is more than just working together; it is a commitment between individuals or organizations to work towards common goals by sharing responsibility, authority, and accountability for results. The purpose of collaboration is to create a shared vision and joint strategies that go beyond the agenda of any of the individual members of the group.

Collaboration is not a defined healthcare discipline, but successful achievement of the social imperative will require systems of care to socialize a formal model for collaboration within and between a patient's health resource-communities.

## *Experience Management*

Relevant and impactful influence over the quality of health of individuals and communities must incorporate their wants and needs and acknowledge that lived experience is their data.

Without this, a system may end up focusing on activities that are more about the needs of the system than those of the individuals and communities it serves.

Healthcare is both an immersive and transformative experience, and everyone who interacts with a patient — whether they be a physician, nurse, pharmacist, greeter, call center, or even janitorial staff — is part of a patient's *health resource community*, in that they are part of the patient's immersive environment and can influence the variables associated with their health status. Understanding that the patient's health resource community extends beyond any one organization is a critical element of experience management.

Some functional elements of experience management include:

o **Anticipatory guidance**

o **Shared decision-making**

o **Shared responsibility**

o **Journey/Thematic mapping**

o **Behavioral values**

For the system to achieve its intent and purpose, each functional requirement has to be accounted for and fulfilled; this determines the nature and scope of the system's operating capabilities.

## Phase 2: Identify and Master Operating Capabilities

Operating capabilities are shaped by how the functional requirements are fulfilled: a bicycle requires fitness and balance; an automobile less so. Operating capabilities must also align with the needs of the infrastructure and operational workflow. There are seven areas of focus for healthcare systems:

## Organizational Capacity

Organizational readiness; structure, governance, and culture aligned with the social imperative; assets, resources, priorities.

## Human Performance/ Workforce

Staffing; roles and responsibilities; training needs; alignment.
Expectations for collaboration and coordination; operational accountability.

## Clinical Process & Operations

Clinical integration and collaboration model; workflows, protocols, programs, and services; quality and outcome measures. Performance achievement model.

## Experience Management

Communication, engagement and activation, shared decision-making, tactile and emotive experience.

## Technology Systems

IT systems, capabilities, feature/function requirements; integration schema infrastructure; configuration, contribution, optimization.

## Data, Analytics and Reporting

Data sources and quality, storage, and management. Analytic and reporting models to meet functional requirements for clinical, operational, and financial performance.

## Finance/Business Models

Value proposition; financial expectations, cost tracking, contracting for value-based goals; ROI model.

In existing organizations, each of these elements requires significant transformational change in order to operationally fulfill the functional requirements. Most have assets that can be repurposed towards the functional requirements. This can be accomplished through a functional asset audit in which assets are evaluated through a new lens. For example, traditional marketing functions might serve the outreach and engagement function in the new systems design.

## Phase 3: Design the Interactions: People, Platforms, Programs, Partners

Improving both the quality of care and the quality of health of target populations takes more than technology; it requires orchestrating and optimizing goal-directed collaboration, operating relationships and knowledge management between the programs, platforms, partners, and personnel that comprise your social imperative infrastructure.

Interaction design is a methodology for managing system-level functionality and performance, with an eye towards care redesign, clinical integration, and revitalizing the experience of care for both patients and professionals.

- o **Tactile performance (e.g., efficiency, consistency, reliability, responsiveness)**
- o **Emotive performance (e.g., dignity, authenticity, integrity, sincerity, urgency)**
- o **Goal-direction, recursive improvement**
- o **Operational and personnel alignment, accountability**
- o **Collaboration and cooperation**
- o **Communications and knowledge sharing**

Our systems of care must develop the capacity to design and orchestrate interactions both within and between systems — people (human systems), platforms (information systems), and places (environmental systems: physical, digital, and virtual) — if we are to achieve the social imperative. Performance metrics should reflect both process and outcomes associated with interaction design.

*14*

# Are We Willing to Learn from the Death of Dr. Susan Moore?

THE DEATH OF Dr. Susan Moore. The death of Dr. Susan Moore. The death of Dr. Susan Moore. Should make our ears ring and blood boil.

Susan Moore was a physician and Black woman who, from her hospital bed, livestreamed her experience of racial bias resulting in her undertreatment, and who, as she predicted, subsequently died of complications from COVID-19.

*Her death is an object lesson in how racism trumps humanity, not just professional identity.*

Medicine failed her, not just because she was a 'fellow physician,' but because we've failed in our practice; her death is an object lesson in how racism trumps humanity, not just professional identity.

The very nature of healthcare practice is tradition: not 'art and science,' but a social construct shaped by history and culture. Training in the healthcare professions is an exercise in submission to authority in order to achieve acceptance: we unconsciously shape our mental models and behavior because it mirrors the thinking and ways of being of those who hold the keys of entry to a world to which we aspire to belong. Subsequent success in practice and academe means sustaining these ways of thinking and acting because they are the benchmarks by which our "competence" — as a member of the community or 'key opinion leader' — is judged. While we like to think these benchmarks are objectively grounded in science, they are susceptible to ideological distortion; pro-attitudes that are shaped by perceived threats or unconscious bias.

Systemic bias is fundamentally exclusionary, but also self-perpetuating and self-protective; the systems themselves are structured to effect and sustain the oppression and discrimination of individuals and groups based on assigned identities. Only systemic change can genuinely eliminate bias.

As long as we put the burden on overcoming racial discrimination on those who are its victims, our society — and economy — will never flourish. There is a limited amount of energy available to us, as individuals and as a society, and if we are socially engineering ourselves to dedicate a substantial proportion of it to sustaining inequities, we are impeding our productive and positive evolution.

Think about all the time and effort we waste — and the damage done to individuals and communities — while we fight over the power to hurt others.

By omission and commission, we invest significant resources to sustain these systemic structures. Our systems of training narrowly define the life stages required for professional maturity, and our systems of practice sustain the forces that shape behavior and subsequent "fit."

We will not achieve true equity of care as long as our systems of training and practice are driven by Euro-centric standards of "respectability" and professional achievement. Our benchmarks for diversity and inclusion must go beyond presence of color but embrace presence of culture. "Inclusion" is more than a seat at the table, but respecting and honoring differences of culture and ethnicity and ensuring that their voice, and its effect, are equitably embedded in decisions made at all levels of society — no matter how uncomfortable it may make people currently in power.

*Our benchmarks for diversity and inclusion must go beyond presence of color but embrace presence of culture.*

# Epilogue

# The Future of Healthcare Was Written Before 1985

I ALWAYS THOUGHT that calculus was a prerequisite for medical school admission because it is said to be the "mathematics of change," and thereby provides an analytic framework to help us understand the dynamic nature of human biology. However, in the years hence, I have come to appreciate that the real value of learning calculus was not in the math, but the framework it provided to help sort out (integrate) the relationships between related concepts, and derive new points of view in the context of another, understood perspective.

This was driven home for me recently as I organized the core set of references — articles and books — for these essays and realized that most of them were written before 1985. Using a reference from the calculus: they have become *functions* in my capacity to understand and manage the changes that have occurred in healthcare in the time since.

Each of these pieces is prescient in its perspective on the challenges facing healthcare today: including, but not limited to, the role of technology in healthcare, clinical decision-making, prevention, social determinants of health, value-based care, professional burnout, medical education, collaboration and teamwork, design thinking, and change management. Not every historical reference remains relevant in its contextually modern era, but these remain extraordinary in their bearing and value to the challenges facing healthcare today.

We live in an era that celebrates the start-up entrepreneur who invents and disrupts, but the fact is that many of the concepts being floated today as new discoveries — like the power of social and behavioral determinants — are just rediscoveries from paths already trod but then grown over from neglect.

Perhaps we have gone too far, encouraging passionate, innovative people to focus on their own ideas, even when they might make a bigger contribution by building their work on the often-strong foundations built by others. For anyone who is working in healthcare policy today, these should be required reading. Here the authors and works are presented in the order I discovered them.

## Neil Postman and Charles Weingartner
*Teaching as a Subversive Activity (New York: Delacorte Press, 1969)*

The introduction to this fifty-year-old critical analysis of our educational system could be rendered relevant today by simply replacing the word "education" with "healthcare."

> *"The thesis of this book is that change —
> constant, accelerated, ubiquitous — is the most striking
> characteristic of the world we live in and that our
> [healthcare] system has not recognized this fact."*

The subtitle says it all: "A no-holds-barred assault on outdated...methods — with dramatic and practical proposals on how [healthcare] can be made relevant to today's world."

Most interesting, in noting a list of problems that are threatening the survival of our society, the seventh sentence of the book notes that "there are more Americans suffering from mental illness than from all other forms of illness combined." In that same paragraph, they note, "the misinformation problem takes on a variety of forms, such as lies, clichés and rumors, and implicates almost everybody, including the President of the United States."

The text, on pursuing relevance and meaning making, deconstructs formal systems of education and makes specific recommendations to develop transformative systems of learning that are relevant to goals of modern society.

## *Jerome Bruner*

*The Process of Education (Cambridge, MA: Harvard University Press, 1960)*

My college mentor — a science educator — had a copy of this thin volume on the shelf above my workspace in his office. It is "an inspiring vision of curiosity and thirst for discovery and knowledge, and its optimistic description of scholars, scientists, teachers and students in a shared intellectual community, and most of all, its generous hopefulness about the possibilities of disciplined and knowledgeable creativity." It was a summary of a conference held at Woods Hole to discuss how education in science might be improved. Again, simply substituting "medicine" for "education" and adding "medical" to the word student would reveal a powerful blueprint for a modern medical school curriculum.

We would all do well to familiarize ourselves with the work of Bruner, a polymath trained as a cognitive psychologist, who did seminal work in developmental science, language development, and our understanding of the interface between the self and the world.

*The Process of Education* defined four critical realms for the design of learning systems that remain especially relevant today as we move away from the mastery of facts and technique to developing skills that will be made to "count in their thinking for the rest of their lives."

I might add that Bruner's *Beyond the Information Given: Studies in the Psychology of Knowing* (Oxford, England: W. W. Norton, 1973) provides an excellent view of the development of mental representations and cognition, adding further to Bruner's potential contribution to how we train physicians in the 21st century.

## George Polya

*How to Solve It: A System of Thinking to Which Can Help You Solve Any Problem (Princeton, NJ: Princeton University Press, 1945)*

Embracing Polya's existing work on problem-solving could have advanced healthcare process improvement by fifty years—his framework is remarkably similar to Plan-Do-Study-Act. It also provides an extraordinary framework for clinical problem-solving; no one should ever use the word "condition" without having read Polya's book; a condition is not a disease, but the current state of the patient in relation to the disease. Throughout my residency, I carried an index card with Polya's heuristics in my bag.

## Norbert Weiner

*The Human Use of Human Beings: Cybernetics and Society (Oxford, England: Houghton Mifflin, 1950)*

While probably the most dated reference in this list, Weiner presents a very optimistic view of what is possible for the role of automation in society, some of which has not been fully realized; and as such, his hopefulness remains fresh. More important, this book predates any current pundit's opinions on the relationship between humans and machines, technologic communication as a social force, and the societal risks of artificial intelligence (which is referenced as automata).

> "...with advances in technology that allow them to learn, the machines may be able to escape human control if humans do not continue proper supervision of them. We might become entirely dependent on them, or even controlled by them. There is danger in trusting decisions to something which cannot think abstractly, and may therefore be unlikely to identify with intellectual human values which are not purely utilitarian."

## George A. Miller

*The Magical Number Seven, Plus or Minus Two: Some*
*Limits on Our Capacity for Processing Information.*
*(Psychological Review. 1956; 63(2): 81–97)*

I discovered this article during medical school, while trying to understand medical problem-solving. One of the most cited papers in psychology, it provides an operational framework for short-term memory, working memory, and human capacity for decision-making. Working memory has an efficacy limit of 7+/- 2 items. The paper also defines the phenomenon of 'chunking' information bits (e.g., seven chunks of seven related items) in order to improve processing power.

Most interesting is that the 1977 book *Medical Problem Solving: An Analysis of Clinical Reasoning* (Cambridge, MA; Harvard University Press, 1977), based on the extensive research and problem-solving simulations conducted by a team led by Arthur Elstein, Lee Shulman, and Sarah Sprafka, came to a similar conclusion: "Clinicians are found to have a distinctly limited capacity for simultaneously considering multiple hypotheses, regardless of the complexity of the problem. Rarely does the number exceed five, and virtually never will an individual be entertaining more than seven."

To my mind, Elstein et al.'s work either replicates or confirms Miller's twenty-one-year-old premises; however, while many of Miller's psychological contemporaries are cited in the book, Miller is not referenced.

## George Engel
*The Need for a New Medical Model: A Challenge for Biomedicine.*
*(Science, 1977; 196(4286): 129–136)*

In 1977, Dr. Engel raised the specter of reductionism in medicine and advocated for a more inclusive scientific model if, as Dr. Engel wrote, "physicians in the future are to apply the same scientific rigor to the approach and understanding of patients and their care as they customarily apply to the diagnosis and treatment of disease." His recommendations were prescient:

> *"The dominant model of disease today is biomedical, and it leaves not room within its framework for the social, psychological and behavioral dimensions of illness. A biopsychosocial model is proposed that provides a blueprint for research, a framework for teaching and a design for action in the real world of healthcare."*

Much of what we consider innovation today would be superfluous if we had taken Dr. Engel's advice to incorporate behavioral dimensions and social factors into our model for care.

## James G. Miller
*Living Systems (New York: McGraw-Hill, 1978)*

A detailed operationalized view of general systems theory as applied to living systems. Provides a 'unified field' approach to health and illness as a function of dynamics within and between our levels of being. This framework provides a whole person view of health and remains germane to current efforts to design integrated systems of care.

## Elliot W. Montroll

*Social dynamics and the quantifying of social forces. (Proceedings of the National Academy of Sciences. 1978; 75(10):4633–4637)*

During medical school, I would occasionally stop in the library and pick up the latest issue of some random journals. This discovery has shaped my thinking for almost four decades. In it, Dr. Montroll proposes a model of social evolution and then tests three laws of social dynamics by tracking the evolutionary process of industrial replacement (e.g., sailing ships vs. steamers; travel by air vs. rail; agricultural to non-agricultural labor force activity). This and other works by Dr. Montroll effectively define a calculus for understanding the evolution of healthcare.

## Ruth E. K. Stein and Dorothy Jessop

*A Noncategorical Approach to Chronic Childhood Illness. (Public Health Reports. 1982; 97(4):354–362)*

I was fortunate to have trained under Dr. Stein, and her work, which was published during my internship, has had an everlasting impact, especially in the modern era of population health, accountable care, and value-based payment reform. This article, and others of hers along the same vein, defines the concept of chronicity as a clinical entity, independent of biomedical or environmental etiology. The critical interaction of disease and behavioral health is clear in these papers, and the idea of a transcendent functional burden of illness remains an open opportunity for novel intervention.

## *Robert S. Gordon*

*An Operational Classification of Disease Prevention.*
*(Public Health Reports. 1983; 98(2): 107–109)*

Dr. Gordon, a renowned public health physician, published this brief report two years before his death. It provides a powerful information architecture and categorization scheme for preventive care planning, with a focus on identifying measures to be "adopted by or practiced on persons not currently feeling the effects of a disease, intended to decrease the risk that that disease will afflict them in the future."

Given the lack of a formal framework for care planning by physicians, the Gordon classification may be just what healthcare needs in the era of value-based care.

# Revised Gordon Care Plan Architecture

| HEALTH-GOAL CATEGORY | Wellness/ Lifestyle | Universal prevention | Selected prevention | Indicated prevention | Condition management | Compassionate care |
|---|---|---|---|---|---|---|
| **OPERATIONAL FOCUS** | Individual focus | Community-based | Characteristic-based | Condition or risk-based | Diagnosis or event-based | Prognosis-based |
| **STRATEGIC TARGETS** | Individuals who seek to achieve or sustain levels of physical, mental, and social well-being, independent of any associated risks or conditions | Targets whole population and aims to prevent or delay universal health risks or conditions | Targets groups or individuals whose risk is above average based on non-medical traits, socio-demographic, or geographic characteristics | Targets groups or individuals with an existing condition or other identifiers indicating condition-related risks | Targets groups or individuals with confirmed diagnosis or other condition with influence over quality of health; focus on improving the condition, or achieving and/or sustaining condition stability | Patients with any serious illness who have physical, functional, psychological, or spiritual distress as a result of their conditions and/ or associated treatments |
| **DETERMINANTS** | Individual choices, preferences, or desires | National or local community membership | Traits such as age, gender, ethnicity, geography | Genetics; anatomy; physiology; neuropsychology; behavior; environment; economics; social factors | Genetics; anatomy; physiology; neuropsychology; behavior; environment; economics; social factors | Individual choices, preferences, or desires in context of symptoms, distress and/or prognosis |
| **EXAMPLES: Goal/ Intervention** | Fitness<br><br>Stress Management<br><br>Nutrition and food choices<br><br>Sleep discipline | Seat belt use<br><br>Weight screening<br><br>Flu shots<br><br>Smoking education | Mammography in women<br><br>Colonoscopy over 50 | CV event reduction in diabetes<br><br>Apnea Screening when BMI>30<br><br>Readmission risk reduction<br><br>Cancer survivorship<br><br>Childhood exposure to ACES | Blood sugar management in DM (pharmacotherapy/ diet)<br><br>Medication management in CHF<br><br>Weight loss in HTN<br><br>Depression management<br><br>Appendicitis/Surgery | Palliative care<br><br>End of life care/ Hospice |

# Appendix 2

# Care Planning Process

**Step 1:** Determine the current state (as defined by physical, informational, and belief variables) of each condition and/or risk factor in each of the care plan categories.

**Step 2:** Compare or benchmark the current state of each condition and/or risk factor against an optimal goal-state for that individual in each of the care plan categories as defined by evidence, best practices, reference standards of the medical community, and/or patient preferences, desires, or aspirations.

**Step 3:** Evaluate the determinants of the current state (including but not limited to molecular, physiologic, structural, neuropsychological, environmental, genomic, biomic, or social), and assess and document their relative influence on the breadth, depth, and scope of variation from goal-state.

**Step 4:** Choose patient-personalized strategies (including but not limited to pharmacotherapy, surgical procedures, behavioral therapies, coaching, human support services, medical devices, and/or social/environmental interventions) to effect change in the patient-specific determinants towards a targeted goal-state. Use patient-level data (including but not limited to clinical, demographic, psychographic, consumer, socio-economic, or educational) to optimize the engagement, acceptance, and commitment to these strategies. For diagnostic processes, pre-determine the optimal scope and sequence of events in order to maximize efficiency and effectiveness of the process.

**Step 5:** Based on the mutually agreed upon strategies, make decisions as to the tactical resources to be deployed — specific medications, procedures, tests, services, amenities, or roles — that are known to support the desired change in the patient's state. Based on the resources deployed, identify and finalize metrics to track progress towards goals and endpoints for the intervention. Wherever possible, escalation paths should be predetermined (e.g., first line to second line therapy) in order to respond efficiently when progress towards goal does not meet expectations.

**Step 6:** Closely monitor the progress towards the goal; if the rate of change does not meet expectations, escalate resources as appropriate. Resources or strategies can be changed, modified, escalated, or de-escalated, as is appropriate for the patient's conditions, needs, or goals for their health.

# References

Abeßer, Jakob, Estefanía Cano, Klaus Frieler, and Martin Pfleiderer. 2014. "Dynamics in Jazz Improvisation – Score-Informed Estimation and Contextual Analysis of Tone Intensities in Trumpet and Saxophone Solos." Paper presented at the 9th Conference on Interdisciplinary Musicology (CIM), Berlin, Germany.

Ader, Jeremy, Christopher J. Stille, David Keller, Benjamin F. Miller, Michael S. Barr, and James M. Perrin. 2015. "The Medical Home and Integrated Behavioral Health: Advancing the Policy Agenda." *Pediatrics* 135, no. 5 (May): 909-17.

Allen, Heidi, and Benjamin D. Sommers. 2019. "Medicaid Expansion and Health: Assessing the Evidence After 5 Years." *JAMA* 322, no. 13 (October): 1253–54.

Allen, Keith D., and Jeffrey F. Hine. 2015. "ABA Applications in the Prevention and Treatment of Medical Problems." In *Clinical and Organizational Applications of Applied Behavior Analysis*, edited by Henry S. Roane, Joel L. Ringdahl, and Terry S. Falcomata, 95-124. San Diego: Academic Press. https://doi.org/10.1016/B978-0-12-420249-8.00005-8.

Artiga, Samantha, Kendal Orgera, and Olivia Pham. 2020. "Disparities in Health and Healthcare: Five Key Questions and Answers." *Kaiser Family Foundation Disparities Brief.* March 4, 2020. https://www.kff.org/disparities-policy/issue-brief/disparities-in-health-and-health-care-five-key-questions-and-answers.

Ballantyne, Helen. 2016. "Developing Nursing Care Plans." *Nursing Standard* 30 (26): 51 –60.

Ballard, David Joseph, Geraldo Ogola, Neil S. Fleming, Dave Heck, Julie Gunderson, Raaj Mehta, Roger Khetan, and Jeffrey D. Kerr. 2008. "The Impact of Standardized Order Sets on Quality and Financial Outcomes." In *Culture and Redesign*, edited by Kerm Henriksen, James B. Battles, Margaret A. Keyes, and Mary L. Grady. Vol. 2 of *Advances in Patient Safety: New Directions and Alternative Approaches.* Rockville, MD: Agency for Healthcare Research and Quality.

Barry, Michael J., and Susan Edgman-Levitan. 2012. "Shared Decision Making — the Pinnacle of Patient-Centered Care." *New England Journal of Medicine* 366 (9): 780-81.

Baxter, Gordon and Ian Sommerville. 2011. "Socio-Technical Systems: From Design Methods to Systems Engineering." *Interacting with Computers* 23, no. 1 (January): 4-17.

Beidelschies, Michelle, Marilyn Alejandro-Rodriguez, Xinge Ji, Brittany Lapin, Patrick Hanaway, and Michael B. Rothberg. 2019. "Association of the Functional Medicine Model of Care with Patient-Reported Health-Related Quality-of-Life Outcomes." *JAMA Network Open* 2, no. 10 (October): e1914017.

Bhatara, Anjali, Anna K. Tirovolas, Lilu Marie Duan, Bianca Levy, and Daniel J. Levitin. 2011. "Perception of Emotional Expression in Musical Performance." *Journal of Experimental Psychology: Human Perception and Performance* 37 (3): 921–34.

Blue Cross Blue Shield. 2017. "Healthy Communities Mean a Better Economy." January 12, 2017. https://www.bcbs.com/the-health-of-america/articles/healthy-communities-mean-better-economy.

Bowen, Judith L. 2006. "Educational Strategies to Promote Clinical Diagnostic Reasoning." *New England Journal of Medicine* 355, no. 21 (November): 2217-25.

Boyd, Cynthia M., Jonathan Darer, Chad Boult, Linda P. Fried, Lisa Boult, Albert W. Wu. 2005. "Clinical Practice Guidelines and Quality of Care for Older Patients with Multiple Comorbid Diseases: Implications for Pay for Performance." *JAMA* 294, no. 6 (August): 716-24.

Bruner, Jerome. 1960. *The Process of Education*. Cambridge, MA: Harvard University Press.

Burland, Karen, and Stephanie Pitts, eds. 2014. *Coughing and Clapping: Investigating Audience Experience*. London: Routledge.

Byrne, Loren. 2007. "Habitat Structure: A Fundamental Concept and Framework for Urban Soil Ecology." *Urban Ecosystems* 10 (3): 255-74.

Centers for Medicare and Medicaid Services. n.d. *Medicare Shared Savings Program Quality Measure Benchmarks for the 2014 and 2015 Reporting Years*. Accessed June 18, 2014. https://www.cms.gov/Medicare/Medicare-Fee-for-Service-Payment/sharedsavingsprogram/Downloads/MSSP-QM-Benchmarks.pdf.

Chang, Rowland W., Georges Bordage, and Karen J. Connell. 1998. "The Importance of Early Problem Representation during Case Presentations." Supplement, *Academic Medicine* 73, no 10: S109-11.

Chapin, Stuart F. III., M.C. Chapin, Pamela A. Matson, and Peter M. Vitousek. 2011. *Principles of Terrestrial Ecosystem Ecology*, 2nd ed. New York: Springer.

Chauhan, Bhupendrasinh F., Maya M. Jeyaraman, Amrinder Singh Mann, Justin Lys, Becky Skidmore, Kathryn M. Sibley, Ahmed M. Abou-Setta, and Ryan Zarychanski. 2017. "Behavior Change Interventions and Policies Influencing Primary Healthcare Professionals' Practice—an Overview of Reviews." *Implementation Science* 12 (3). https://www.ncbi.nlm.nih.gov/pmc/articles/ PMC5216570/.

Cheron, Daniel M., Jill T. Ehrenreich, and Donna B. Pincus. 2009. "Assessment of Parental Experiential Avoidance in a Clinical Sample of Children with Anxiety Disorders." *Child Psychiatry and Human Development* 40, no. 3 (September): 383-403.

Cooper, John O., Timohy E. Heron, and William L. Heward. 2007. *Applied Behavior Analysis*. 2nd ed. Upper Saddle River, NJ: Pearson. https://www.pearson.com/us/higher-education/program/Cooper-Applied-Behavior-Analysis-2nd-Edition/PGM94828.html.

"County Health Rankings." 2020. County Health Rankings & Roadmaps (website). March 10, 2020. https://www.countyhealthrankings.org/app/newyork/2020/rankings/outcomes/overall.

Crowley, Ryan A., and Neil Kirschner. 2015. "The Integration of Care for Mental Health, Substance Abuse, and Other Behavioral Health Conditions into Primary Care: An American College of Physicians Position Paper." *Annals of Internal Medicine* 163, no. 4 (August): 298–99. http://annals.org/aim/fullarticle/2362310/integration-care-mental-health-substance-abuse-other-behavioral-health-conditions.

Danese, Andrea, and Bruce S. McEwen. 2012. "Adverse Childhood Experiences, Allostasis, Allostatic Load, and Age-Related Disease." *Physiology and Behavior* 106, no. 1 (April): 29–39.

DellaSala Dominick A., and Chad T. Hanson, eds. 2015. *The Ecological Importance of Mixed-Severity Fires: Nature's Phoenix*. New York: Elsevier.

Dillenburger, Karola, and Mickey Keenan. 2009. "None of the As in ABA Stand for Autism: Dispelling the Myths." *Journal of Intellectual & Developmental Disability* 34, no 2 (June): 193-195. https:// www.tandfonline.com/ doi/full/10.1080/13668250902845244.

Ding, Wei, Xia Lin, and Michael Zarro. 2010. *Information Architecture: The Design and Integration of Information Spaces*. San Rafael, CA: Morgan & Claypool.

Eckert, Regina, Michael West, David Altman, Katy Steward, and Bill Pasmore. 2014. *Delivering a Collective Leadership Strategy for Healthcare*. London: Centre for Creative Leadership; The Kings Fund.

Eerola, Tuomas, Anders Friberg, and Roberto Bresin. 2013. "Emotional Expression in Music: Contribution, Linearity, and Additivity of Primary Musical Cues." *Frontiers in Psychology* 4: 487.

Engel GL. 1977. "The Need for a New Medical Model: A Challenge for Biomedicine." *Science* 196 (4286): 129–36.

Fairhurst Merle T., Petr Janata, and Peter E. Keller. 2014. "Leading the Follower: An fMRI Investigation of Dynamic Cooperativity and Leader-Follower Strategies in Synchronization with an Adaptive Virtual Partner." *Neuroimage* 84 (January): 688-97.

Fredrickson, Lief. 2016. "The Surprising Link Between Postwar Suburban Development and Today's Inner-City Lead Poisoning." February 26, 2016. https://www.govtech.com/fs/The-Surprising-Link-Between-Postwar-Suburban-Development-and-Todays-Inner-City-Lead-Poisoning.html.

Friedrich, Tamara L., William B. Vessey, Matthew J. Schuelke, Gregory A. Ruark, and Michael D. Mumford. 2009. "A Framework for Understanding Collective Leadership: The Selective Utilization of Leader and Team Expertise within Networks." *Leadership Quarterly* 20, no. 6 (December): 933-58.

Galenson, David W. 2009. *Conceptual Revolutions in Twentieth-Century Art.* Cambridge: Cambridge University Press.

Gallant, Mary P., Meaghan Tartaglia, Susan Hardman, and Kara Burke. 2019. "Using Tai Chi to Reduce Fall Risk Factors among Older Adults: An Evaluation of a Community-Based Implementation." *Journal of Applied Gerontology* 38, no. 7 (July): 983–98.

Geronimus, Arline T. 2001. "Understanding and Eliminating Racial Inequalities in Women's Health in the United States: The Role of the Weathering Conceptual Framework." *Journal of the American Medical Women's Association* 56:133–36, 149–50.

Geronimus, Arline T., John Bound, Timothy A. Waidmann, Cynthia G. Colen, and Dianne Steffick. 2001. "Inequality in Life Expectancy, Functional Status, and Active Life Expectancy across Selected Black and White Populations in the United States." *Demography* 38 (2): 227–51.

Geronimus, Arline T., John Bound, Timothy A. Waidmann, Marianne M. Hillemeier, and Patricia B. Burns. 1996. "Excess Mortality among Blacks and Whites in the United States." *New England Journal of Medicine* 335:1552–58.

Geronimus, Arline T., Margaret Hicken, Danya Keene, and John Bound. 2006. "'Weathering' and Age Patterns of Allostatic Load Scores among Blacks and Whites in the United States." *American Journal of Public Health* 96, no. 5 (May): 826-33.

Gloor, Peter A. 2006. *Swarm Creativity: Competitive Advantage through Collaborative Innovation Networks.* New York: Oxford University Press.

Godbold, J.A., M.T. Bulling, and M. Solan. 2011. "Habitat Structure Mediates Biodiversity Effects on Ecosystem Properties." *Proceedings of the Royal Society B: Biological Sciences* 278 (1717): 2510 - 18.

Goings, Sherri, and Charles Ofria. 2009. "Ecological Approaches to Diversity Maintenance in Evolutionary Algorithm." In *2009 IEEE Symposium on Artificial Life,* 124–130. Piscataway, NJ: Institute of Electrical and Electronic Engineers.

Goodson Leigh, and Matt Vassar. 2011. "An Overview of Ethnography in Healthcare and Medical Education Research." *Journal of Educational Evaluation for Health Professions* 8:1–5.

Gordon, R.S., Jr. 1983. "An Operational Classification of Disease Prevention." *Public Health Reports* 98 (2): 107–109.

Green, Elizabeth A.H. 1997. *The Modern Conductor*. 6th ed. United Kingdom: Prentice Hall.

Grinberger, A. Yair. 2019. "Weighting the Effects of Spatial Cognition and Activity Anchors on Time–Space Activity." *The Professional Geographer* 71 (1): 52-64.

Hannah, Lauren A. 2015. "Stochastic Optimization." In *International Encyclopedia of the Social & Behavioral Sciences*, 2nd ed., edited by James A. Wright, 473-81. New York: Elsevier.

Heath, Sarah. 2018. "Intermountain Alliance to Address Social Determinants of Health." PatientEngagementHIT (website). Updated July 5, 2018. https://patientengagementhit.com/news/intermountain-alliance-to-address-social-determinants-of-health.

Heffernan, Robert, and Steve LaValle. 2006. "Advocacy in the Customer Focused Enterprise: The Next Generation of CRM Done Right." *IBM Global Business Services Executive Handbook*. ftp://public.dhe.ibm.com/software/emea/dk/frontlines/Advocacyinthecustomer-SFM.pdf.

Hibbard, Judith H., and Jessica Greene. 2013. "What the Evidence Shows about Patient Activation: Better Health Outcomes and Care Experiences; Fewer Data on Costs." *Health Affairs* 32, no. 2 (February): 207-14.

Hood, Carlyn M., Keith P. Gennuso, Geoffrey R. Swain, and Bridget B. Catlin. 2016. "County Health Rankings: Relationships between Determinant Factors and Health Outcomes." *American Journal of Preventive Medicine* 50, no. 2 (February): 129-35.

Howell, Junia, Sara Goodkind, Leah Jacobs, Dominique Branson, and Elizabeth Miller. 2019. "Pittsburgh's Inequality across Gender and Race." *Gender Analysis White Papers. City of Pittsburgh's Gender Equity Commission.* Published September 17, 2019. https://apps.pittsburghpa.gov/redtail/ images/7109_Pittsburgh's_Inequality_Across_Gender_and_Race_09_18_19.pdf.

Jackson, George L., Benjamin J. Powers, Ranee Chatterjee, Janet Prvu Bettger, Alex R. Kemper, Vic Hasselblad, Rowena J. Dolor et al. 2013. "The Patient-Centered Medical Home: A Systematic Review." *Annals of Internal Medicine* 158 (3): 169-178.

Katch, Hannah. 2017. "Medicaid Works: Millions Benefit from Medicaid's Effective, Efficient Coverage." Center on Budget and Policy Priorities (website). June 2, 2017. https://www.cbpp.org/research/ health/medicaid-works-millions-benefit-from-medicaids-effective-efficient-coverage.

Kazdin, Alan E. 2007. *Behavior Modification in Applied Settings.* 7th ed. Long Grove, IL: Waveland Press. https://www.waveland.com/browse.php?t=369.

Keller, Peter E. 2008. "Joint Action in Music Performance." In *Enacting Intersubjectivity: A Cognitive and Social Perspective on the Study of Interactions,* edited by F. Morganti, A. Carassa, and G. Riva, 205-21. Emerging Communication: Studies on New Technologies and Practices in Communication, vol. 10. Amsterdam: IOS Press.

Keller, Peter E. 2012. "Mental Imagery in Music Performance: Underlying Mechanisms and Potential Benefits." *Annals of the New York Academy of Sciences* 1252, no. 1 (April): 206-13.

Keller, Peter E. 2014. "Ensemble Performance: Interpersonal Alignment of Musical Expression." In *Expressiveness in Music Performance: Empirical Approaches Across Styles and Cultures*, edited by Doryotta Fabian, Renee Timmers, and Emery Schubert, 260–82. New York: Oxford University Press.

Keltner, Dacher, and Jonathan Haight. 1999. "Social Functions of Emotions at Four Levels of Analysis." *Cognition and Emotion* 13 (5): 505-21.

Khalifa, Mohammed and Kathy Ning Shen. 2006. "Effects of Knowledge Representation on Knowledge Acquisition and Problem Solving." *Electronic Journal of Knowledge Management* 4, no. 2 (March): 153-58.

Khan, Numan, Francoise A. Marvel, Jane Wang, and Seth S. Martin. 2017. "Digital Health Technologies to Promote Lifestyle Change and Adherence." *Current Treatment Options in Cardiovascular Medicine* 19 (8): 60. https://link.springer.com/article/10.1007%2Fs11936-017-0560-4.

Klein, J.T. 2014. "Interdisciplinary Teamwork: The Dynamics of Collaboration and Integration." In *Interdisciplinary Collaboration: An Emerging Cognitive Science*, edited by Sharon J. Derry, Christian D. Schunn, and Morton Ann Gernsbacker. n.p.: Psychology Press.

Kubina, Richard M. and Kirsten K.L. Yurick. 2012. *The Precision Teaching Book.* Lemont, PA: Greatness Achieved Publishing Company.

Lamont, Alexandra. 2012. "Emotion, Engagement and Meaning in Strong Experiences of Music Performance." *Psychology of Music* 40 (5): 574–94.

Lepš, Jan, and Marcel Rejmánek. 1991. "Convergence or Divergence: What Should We Expect from Vegetation Succession?" *Oikos* 62, no.2 (November): 261-64.

Linden, Russ. 2003. "The Discipline of Collaboration." *Leader to Leader.* 2003, no. 29 (Summer): 41-47.

Lopez-Casasnovas Guillem, Berta Rivera, and Luis Currais, eds. 2005. *Health and Economic Growth: Findings and Policy Implications.* Cambridge, MA: MIT Press.

Lorenz, Konrad: 1973. *Behind the Mirror: A Search for a Natural History of Human Knowledge.* New York: Harcourt Brace Jovanovich.

Losos, Jonathan B. 2011. "Convergence, Adaptation, and Constraint." *Evolution* 65, no. 7 (July): 1827-40.

Lucas, Franc. 2018. "Techniques for Empathy Interviews in Design Thinking." Envato Tuts+ (website). June 26, 2018. https://webdesign.tutsplus.com/articles/techniques-of-empathy-interviews-in-design-thinking--cms-31219.

Manatt, Phelps & Phillips, LLP. 2019. "Medicaid's Impact on Healthcare Access, Outcomes and State Economies." *Robert Wood Johnson Foundation Briefing Series: Key Medicaid Issues for New State Policymakers.* February 1, 2019. https://www.rwjf.org/en/library/research/2019/02/medicaid-s-impact-on-health-care-access-outcomes-and-state-economies.html.

Mauceri, John. 2019. *For the Love of Music: A Conductor's Guide to the Art of Listening.* New York: Alfred A. Knopf.

McEwen, Bruce S., and Teresa Seeman. 1999. "Protective and Damaging Effects of Mediators of Stress: Elaborating and Testing the Concepts of Allostasis and Allostatic Load." *Annals of the New York Academy of Sciences* 896, no. 1 (December): 30–47.

Merahn, Steven. 2015. "Knowledge Representation and Care Planning for Population Health Management." *Journal of Medical Practice Management* 31, no. 2 (August): 126-30.

Montroll, Elliott W. 1978. "Social Dynamics and the Quantifying of Social Forces." *Proceedings of the National Academy of Sciences of the United States of America* 75, no. 10 (October): 4633–37.

Mostashari, Farzad, Darshak Sanghavi, and Mark McClellan. 2014. "Health Reform and Physician-Led Accountable Care: The Paradox of Primary Care Physician Leadership." *JAMA Network* 311 (18): 1855-56.

Mrazek, Patricia J., and Robert J. Haggerty, eds. 1994. *Reducing Risks for Mental Disorders: Frontiers for Preventive Intervention Research*. Washington, DC: National Academy Press.

Mutnick, Andrew, and Michael Barone. 2014. "Assessing and Remediating Clinical Reasoning." In *Remediation in Medical Education*, edited by Adina Kalet and Calvin L. Chou, 85-101. New York: Springer.

New York Public Interest Research Group. 2014. *The Doctor Is In: New York's Increasing Number of Doctors*. August 21, 2014. https://www.nypirg.org/pubs/health/2014.08.21DoctorIsIn.pdf.

Norman, Don A., Jim Miller, and Austin Henderson. 1995. "What You See, Some of What's in the Future, and How We Go about Doing It: HI at Apple Computer." In *CHI'95: Conference Companion on Human Factor in Computing Systems*, edited by I. Katz, R. Mack, and L. Marks, 155. New York: Association for Computing Machinery.

Office of Disease Prevention and Health Promotion. n.d. "Healthy People 2020: Social Determinants of Health, Office of Disease Prevention and Health Promotion." Site last modified October 8, 2020. https://www. healthypeople.gov/ 2020/topics-objectives/topic/ social-determinants-of-health.

Porter, Michael E. 2010. "What is Value in Healthcare?" *New England Journal of Medicine* 363 (December): 2477-81.

Powell, Warren B. 2011. *Approximate Dynamic Programming: Solving the Curses of Dimensionality.* 2nd ed. Hoboken, NJ: Wiley-Blackwell / John Wiley & Sons.

Powell, Warren B. 2019. "A Unified Framework for Stochastic Optimization." *European Journal of Operational Research* 275, no. 3 (June): 795-821.

Powell, Warren B. Forthcoming. *Stochastic Optimization and Learning: A Unified Framework.* Hoboken, NJ: John Wiley & Sons.

Pullman, Madeleine E., and Michael Gross. 2004. "Ability of Experience Design Elements to Elicit Emotions and Loyalty Behaviors." *Decision Sciences* 35, no. 3 (August): 551-78.

Rakel, David. 2017. *Integrative Medicine.* 4th ed. Philadelphia, PA: Saunders Elsevier.

Relman, Arnold S. 1980. "The New Medical-Industrial Complex." *New England Journal of Medicine* 303 (October): 963-70.

Roane Henry S., Joel E. Ringdahl, and Terry Falcomata eds. 2015. *Clinical and Organizational Applications of Applied Behavior Analysis.* San Diego: Academic Press, San Diego. https://www.elsevier.com/books/clinical-and-organizational-applications-of-applied-behavior-analysis/roane/978-0-12-420249-8.

Scherer, Klaus R., and Eduardo Coutinho. 2013. "How Music Creates Emotion: A Multifactorial Process Approach." In *The Emotional Power of Music: Multidisciplinary Perspectives on Musical Arousal, Expression, and Social Control*, edited by Tom Cochrane, Bernardino Fantini, and Klaus R. Scherer, 121–45. New York: Oxford University Press.

Scherer, Klaus R., and Marcel R. Zentner. 2001. "Emotional Effects of Music: Production Rules." In *Music and Emotion: Theory and Research (Series in Affective Science)*, edited by Patrick N. Juslin and John A. Sloboda, 361–92. New York: Oxford University Press.

Schoen, Cathy, Robin Osborn, David Squires, Michelle Doty, Roz Pierson, and Sandra Applebaum. 2011. "New 2011 Survey of Patients with Complex Care Needs in Eleven Countries Finds That Care is Often Poorly Coordinated." *Health Affairs* 30, no. 12 (December): 2437-48.

Shorck, Nicholas J. 2015. "Personalized Medicine: Time for One-Person Trials." *Nature* 520, no. 7549 (April): 609-11. https://www.nature.com/news/personalized-medicine-time-for-one-person-trials-1.17411.

Schroeder, Steven A. 2007. "We Can Do Better— Improving the Health of the American People." *New England Journal of Medicine* 357 (September): 1221-28. https://www.nejm.org/doi/pdf/ 10.1056/NEJMsa073350.

Sloboda, John A., and Patrick N. Juslin. 2001. "Psychological Perspectives on Music and Emotion." In *Music and Emotion: Theory and Research (Series in Affective Science)*, edited by Patrick N. Juslin and John A. Sloboda, 71–104. New York: Oxford University Press.

Sowa, J.F., and J.A. Zachman. 1992. "Extending and Formalizing the Framework for Information Systems Architecture." *IBM Systems Journal* 31 (3): 590-616.

Stein, Ruth E.K., and Dorothy Jones Jessop. 1982. "A Noncategorical Approach to Chronic Childhood Illness." *Public Health Reports* 97, no. 4 (July-August): 354–62.

Stein, Ruth E.K., and Dorothy Jones Jessop. 1989. "What Diagnosis Does Not Tell: The Case for a Noncategorical Approach to Chronic Illness in Childhood." *Social Science & Medicine* 29 (6): 769–78.

Timmers, Renee, Jennifer Macritchie, Siobhan M. Schabrun, Tribikram Thapa, Manuel Varlet, and Peter E. Keller. 2020. "Neural Multimodal Integration Underlying Synchronization with a Co-Performer in Music: Influences of Motor Expertise and Visual Information." *Neuroscience Letters* 721:134803. https://doi.org/10.1016/j.neulet.2020.134803.

Tran Viet-Thai, Caroline Barnes, Victor M. Montori, Bruno Falissard, and Philippe Ravaud. 2015. "Taxonomy of the Burden of Treatment: A Multi-Country Web-Based Qualitative Study of Patients with Chronic Conditions." *BMC Medicine* 13:115.

Wilson, Edward O. 2014. *The Meaning of Human Existence.* New York: W.W. Norton.

Winfield, L., K. DeSalvo, and D. Muhlestein. 2018. *Social Determinants Matter, but Who is Responsible?* Salt Lake City, Utah: Leavitt Partners. https://leavittpartners. com/whitepaper/social-determinants-matter-but-who-is-responsible.

Wong, Connie, Samuel L. Odom, Kara Hume, Ann W. Cox, Angel Fettig, Suzanne Kucharczyk, Matthew E. Brock, Joshua B. Plavnick, Veronica P. Fleury, and Tia R. Schultz. 2014. *Evidence-Based Practices for Children, Youth, and Young Adults with Autism Spectrum Disorder.* Chapel Hill: The University of North Carolina, Frank Porter Graham Child Development Institute, Autism Evidence-Based Practice Review Group. http:// autismpdc.fpg.unc.edu/sites/autismpdc.fpg.unc.edu/ files/2014-EBP-Report.pdf.

Yousif, Hisham, Nworah Ayogu, and Taison Bell. 2020. "The Path Forward - An Antiracist Approach to Academic Medicine." *New England Journal of Medicine* 383, no. 15 (October): e91.

Zachman, John A. 1987. "A Framework for Information Systems Architecture." *IBM Systems Journal,* 38 (2.3): 454-70.

# About the Author

STEVEN MERAHN IS the author of *Care Evolution*, based on his 40-plus years of wildly diverse experience working across almost the entire healthcare ecosystem: in public health, strategic communications and media, information services and technology, health systems and integrated delivery networks, health plans, clinical practice, population health, and value-based care.

Dr. Merahn's non-traditional career as a physician-executive has provided him deep, hands-on, experience with strategic planning, design and development of programs and services, managing operations, effecting change, and managing innovation. He has brought those skills to publicly traded global multi-national corporations, private equity backed middle-market companies, non-profit and mission-driven organizations, and start-ups, as well as his own entrepreneurial and charitable ventures. He has worked for and with some of the world's largest companies and well-known brands, urban and rural care delivery systems, multi-state provider networks, and in government.

A graduate of the Albert Einstein College of Medicine, Dr. Merahn is a physician by training, but also an artist, craftsman, educator, and parent. His work has always taken place at boundaries between diverse, and not always apparently related, disciplines; he has a unique portfolio of experience, including instructional design, social anthropology, Agile software development, behavioral economics, data science, psychoanalysis, and dramaturgy. An intellectual adventurer, his interest in medicine was less about a calling as a clinician and more about a deep desire to understand the human experience and a passion for human service: mastering the complexities of humanness afforded him a level of understanding and skills which supported his goal to help people realize their full potential, improve the human condition, and elevate civil society. He believes that health is only one component of that potential: we cannot discount the power and value of art, music, theater, craftsmanship, philosophy, literature, cognitive science, social policy, discrete mathematics, and a host of other disciplines that serve as critical success factors in any individual's sense of comfort, fit, or satisfaction in their lives — both personal and professional.

He is a vocal advocate for equity and inclusion in civil society, the power of the "human-factor" in our systems of care, and believes in the principles of personal integrity, relentless intellectual vigor, generosity, forgiveness, courage, commitment, and play.

Join the Care Evolution at www.thecareevolution.com